HOW TO CHEAT

AT

Cleaning

HOW TO CHEAT

AT

Cleaning

**Time-Slashing Techniques to Cut Corners
and Restore Your Sanity**

JEFF BREDENBERG

The Taunton Press

The Taunton Press

The Taunton Press, Inc., 63 South Main Street, PO Box 5506, Newtown, CT 06470-5506
e-mail: tp@taunton.com

Editor: Pamela Hoenig/Erica Sanders-Foege
Cover design: Howard Grossman
Front cover: Photo by Jeffrey Krein
Illustrator: Joel Holland

Library of Congress Cataloging-in-Publication Data
Bredenberg, Jeff.
  How to cheat at cleaning : time-slashing techniques to cut corners and restore your sanity /
Jeff Bredenberg.
     p. cm.
  Includes bibliographical references and index.
  ISBN-13: 978-1-56158-870-1 (alk. paper)
  ISBN-10: 1-56158-870-9 (alk. paper)
  1. House cleaning. I. Title.

TX324.B744 2007
648'.5--dc22

                              2006023879

Printed in the United States of America
10 9 8 7 6 5 4 3 2 1

FOR GLADYS BREDENBERG.

Mom, maybe you shouldn't read any further.

ACKNOWLEDGMENTS

The author is grateful for the invaluable expertise of the following sources:

Shannon Ackley
professional organizer,
Shelton, Connecticut

Jennifer Armentrout
test kitchen manager
and recipe editor for *Fine
Cooking* magazine,
Newtown, Connecticut

Alexander Barco
service technician, Computer
Medic, Dublin, Pennsylvania

Chris Barry
engineer for specialty glass
manufacturer Pilkington,
Toledo, Ohio

Sandra Beckwith
writer and speaker on gender
differences and male behavior,
author of *Why Can't a Man
Be More Like a Woman?*,
Fairport, New York

Steve Boorstein
a.k.a. The Clothing Doctor,
author of *The Ultimate Guide
to Shopping and Caring
for Clothing* and proprietor of
www.clothingdoctor.com,
Glen Echo, Maryland

Boy Scout Troop 320
in the suburbs of
Philadelphia, Pennsylvania

Pamela Brown, Ph.D
professor at the Texas
Cooperative Extension, Texas
A&M University, Lubbock, Texas

Cynthia Braun
professional organizer,
Lake Grove, New York

Dorothy Burling
retiree, Mishawaka, Indiana

C. Lee Cawley
professional organizer,
Alexandria, Virginia

Alan Cook
entrepreneur, inventor of
self-cleaning cat litter box,
Chicago, Illinois

Rashelle Cooper
product buyer for PetSmart,
Phoenix, Arizona

Pamela Dalton, Ph.D
odor scientist, Monell
Chemical Senses Center,
Philadelphia, Pennsylvania

Jeff Dross
product manager and trend
analyst for Kichler Lighting,
Cleveland, Ohio

Mary Findley
president, Mary Moppins Co.,
Eugene, Oregon

Evan Galen
architect, New York City

Charles Gerba, Ph.D
microbiologist at the
University of Arizona, Tucson

Joe Grant
owner, Computer Medic,
Dublin, Pennsylvania

Tom Gustin
product manager for Merry
Maids cleaning service,
Memphis, Tennessee

Elizabeth Hagen
professional organizer,
Sioux Falls, South Dakota

Rachel Hepner
spokesperson for specialty
glass manufacturer Pilkington,
Toledo, Ohio

Joni Hilton
creator of Holy Cow
cleaning products,
Sacramento, California

Roy Hinrichs
Internet technology manager,
Fort Worth, Texas

Jon Hoch
founder, Pressure Washers
Direct, Romeoville, Illinois

Ingrid Johnson
professor at the Fashion
Institute of Technology in
New York City

Kerul Kassel
productivity consultant,
Saint Cloud, Florida

Dana Korey
professional organizer,
Del Mar, California

Alexandra Krost
film crew worker,
Richmond, Virginia

Melissa Laiserin
dog behavior expert for
PetSmart, Phoenix, Arizona

Alisa LeSueur
executive director of the
American Association of Rain
Carrying System Installation
Specialists, San Antonio, Texas

Alexandria Lighty
owner, House Doctors Handyman Service, New York City

Robert R. Matheson, Ph.D.
technical manager for strategic
technology for DuPont Performance Coatings, Troy, Michigan

Janet Nelson
a Ross, Iowa-based spokesperson for The Maids Home Services

Susan Newman, Ph.D.
social psychologist at Rutgers University, author of *The Book of No: 250 Ways to Say It—and Mean It*, Metuchen, New Jersey

Lindsay Peroff
spokesperson for 1-800-GOT-JUNK?, Vancouver, British Columbia, Canada

Lisa Peterson
Newton, Connecticut-based spokesperson for the American Kennel Club

J. Winston Porter, Ph.D.
president of the Waste Policy Center consulting organization in Leesburg, Virginia, and former assistant administrator of the Environmental Protection Agency

Jay M. Portnoy, M.D.
chief of allergy, asthma, and immunology at the Children's Mercy Hospital, Kansas City, Missouri

Charlotte Reed
pet care expert, New York City

Philip Reed
senior consumer advice editor for Edmunds.com, Santa Monica, California

Trey Rogers, Ph.D.
professor of turf grass management, Michigan State University, East Lansing, Michigan.

Brian Sansoni
vice president of the Soap and Detergent Association, Washington, DC.

Victoria Scarborough, Ph.D.
director of research and development for Thompson's Water Seal, Olive Branch, Mississippi

Pat Schweitzer
senior home economist for Reynolds Consumer Products, Richmond, Virginia

Alissa Shanley
landscape and garden designer, Denver, Colorado.

Courtney Shaver
public relations coordinator, the Container Store, Coppell, Texas

Jen Singer
parenting writer and a stay-at-home mom, Kinnelon, New Jersey

Erik Sjogren
senior brand manager for Dixie Tabletop, Atlanta, Georgia.

Sarah Smock
spokesperson for Merry Maids cleaning service, Memphis, Tennessee

Judi Sturgeon
professional house cleaner and home health aid, Ambler, Pennsylvania

Brad Turner
plant manager for the Communications Factory, Mantua, Ohio

Lance Walheim
Exeter, California–based horticulturalist and garden expert for Bayer Advanced lawn care and pest control products company

Deborah Wiener
interior designer, Silver Spring, Maryland

Jeff Zbar
a.k.a. The Chief Home Officer, home office consultant, Coral Springs, Florida

*

The author would like to acknowledge the following print sources and those associated with them:

Consumer Reports, a valuable source of expert guidance about products.

Susan Strasser for her inspiring, scholarly history of American housework, *Never Done.*

Tim Vine of the newspaper *The Scotsman,* for his slightly less scholarly but nevertheless inspiring account of how to make your bed without getting out of it.

*

The author also is grateful for the contributions of executive editor Pam Hoenig, assistant editor Katie Benoit, the rest of the staff at The Taunton Press, and agent Linda Konner.

~ CONTENTS ~

PERFECTIONISM IS SO OVERRATED

I'm the kind of person who's dying to dust the house with a leaf blower. I compile lists of things you can clean in the dishwasher—beside dishes. I'm a disciple of Erma Bombeck, the wry columnist who penned the words, "Housework, if you do it right, will kill you."

Do I want to be a slave to my house, working my fingers raw to create a shimmering show palace? No. Just give me an orderly, presentable, and sanitary environment. But don't make me work too hard for it—I have a career, you know, dinner to get on the table, and Little League games to attend. To heck with perfectionism. I'm gonna cheat.

What exactly do I mean by "cheating at cleaning"? If there's a faster way to clean, I'm going to adopt it. If corners can be cut, I'm going to cut them. If technology offers more cleaning power, automated cleaning, and easy-care materials, I'm there. And I'm going to set my own standards for cleanliness—goals that may be somewhat south of Martha Stewart's.

These actually are exciting times for people who hate to clean. Nanotech materials—that is, materials designed for specific purposes, molecule by molecule—have begun to reach the market. While few such products are in wide circulation yet, the science has given us miracle microfiber cleaning cloths, window glass that cleans itself, and light bulbs that destroy odor-causing particles. Self-cleaning garments aren't far behind. Personally, I'm hoping for dinner plates that scrape themselves off and jump into the dishwasher.

This talk of products leads me to a couple of crucial points about the writing of this book. First, many people who want to cheat at cleaning also hope to do so for minimal cost. Rest assured that for every innovative product I mention, there are 20 ways to cut corners that don't involve extra expense at all. Second, it's impossible to give specific advice without the occasional mention of brand names. I want you to know that I accepted no freebies from manufacturers when I researched this book; I bought all of my own products for testing and I don't sell these products either.

Speaking of research, you'll notice that this book is written in a unique way. As I hunted for the cheatingest shortcuts possible, I spoke with scores of experts who were generous with advice. I name them in the text because I want to acknowledge them and because I want you to appreciate the authority of the information and the freshness of this research.

I also hope you find this book as fun to read as it was for me to write. The core of this book is specific advice on how to cheat at cleaning. However, along the way you'll also hear about the junk-removal company that had to dispose of 13 enormous Buddha statues. The guy who washed his socks in the dishwasher (honest, I don't do that). The couple who use their robotic vacuum cleaner to serve beer to guests. The researcher who bought dirty underwear from his students—all in the name of science.

My final point is an invitation to you. Not every person I quote has an impressive string of letters after his or her name. I'll be writing about home management for a long while, and I welcome tips and feedback from savvy readers such as yourself. Please feel free to write to me in care of this publisher, or stop in at www.jeffbredenberg.com and provide your input over the Internet. I may not put your name in lights, but I'll be happy to brand you as a first-class cheater.

—Jeff Bredenberg

REWRITING THE RULES YOUR
MOTHER TAUGHT YOU

We all know what happened as two-career couples became the norm over the last several decades: Scores of new duties came rushing onto our to-do lists like a tsunami. In days of yore, Ozzie-and-Harriet families had one adult who went into the world to make money and another who managed the home front. Today, most families would collapse without two incomes.

With that as a backdrop, consider this interesting bit of research from the Soap and Detergent Association: 62 percent of women say they clean their homes pretty much the same way their mothers did. For goodness sake, corporations took a wrecking ball to the rules of business, but we're using the same old 1950s rules to manage our homes? No wonder we're overwhelmed. No wonder we're all going crazy.

It's time to rewrite the rules your mother taught you for housecleaning. Nothing less than your sanity is at stake.

One of the hardest things to set aside will be perfectionism. Why? Because we are inundated with images from movies, television, and magazines depicting homes with clutter-free, glimmering countertops—places where upholstery and dog hair never meet, where dust bunnies are extinct. Such homes are not achievable in the real world. Even when we work hard at house-cleaning, we feel guilty that we're not meeting unreachable goals. Let's wipe the slate clean and substitute a new set of priorities that meets the needs of modern families—a change that will restore your mental health.

GOAL 1: KEEP A SAFE AND HEALTHY HOME If you have to choose between killing germs and dusting your Hummels®, kill the germs. *How to Cheat at Cleaning* shows you how you can easily sanitize in all the right places.

GOAL 2: BE ABLE TO FIND YOUR POSSESSIONS WHEN YOU NEED THEM If your system's functional, it's fine. For those of you still in search of a semblance of order, this book provides scores of easy de-cluttering techniques.

GOAL 3: KEEP THE KIND OF HOME YOU ARE HAPPY WITH You are the one who has to be pleased with your surroundings, not your mother or your next-door neighbor.

> ### NEW RULES FOR CLEANING

New goals require new pathways for reaching them and a new mind-set. Rather than perpetually marching toward perfection, we need real-world approaches—corner-cutting, time-saving, minimal-effort techniques for cleaning. Yes, we need ways of *cheating*.

The new rules for doing this are divided into two categories: mind-set, to get you properly focused, and procedures, to make sure you expend no more time or energy than absolutely necessary. These general principles will serve as valuable background as you proceed to all the specific corner-cutting advice in the coming chapters.

YOUR CHEATIN' HEART

Just what is it you spend so much time cleaning? Your material possessions. By redefining your whole approach to ownership, you can seriously reduce the time and effort you devote to cleaning. Here are some rules to put you into the cheat-at-cleaning frame of mind.

BE BRAVE ENOUGH TO THROW THINGS OUT Some of us actually have trouble throwing stuff away even when it's worn out, beyond repair, and has no conceivable value to anyone. I contend you should dispose of possessions that are in good repair, too, if you haven't used them within the last year. This goes for clothing, appliances, kitchenware, and more. Few of us have the extra physical and mental capacity to manage these unproductive items that clutter our homes.

BE WILLING TO SPEND MONEY IN EXCHANGE FOR CONVENIENCE Tolerance for spending varies from one individual to another, but remember that convenience items virtually allow you to "buy" time—often for a surprisingly small cost. Keep in mind also that any cleaning challenge is an invitation—I say *outright permission*—to buy cool gear.

ACQUIRE THE RIGHT STUFF, LITTLE BY LITTLE Your wardrobe is probably rife with clothes that stain easily, wrinkle readily, or require special care, such as hand washing and dry cleaning. Cumulatively, these clothes are an enormous hidden burden in your life. But no one expects you to toss them all out today. Just make sure that you replace worn-out clothes with stain- and wrinkle-resistant ones—items you can pull out of the dryer, hang, and wear without further care. This Materials On a Program (MOP) philosophy applies to virtually everything you own—not only clothing but also furniture, flooring, vehicles, appliances, building materials, and more. When it's time to buy something new, make easy care and easy cleaning priorities in your decision.

DON'T BUY THINGS THAT CAUSE YOU ANXIETY Do you have a car that's so pricey you feel compelled to wash and wax it

10 THINGS YOU CAN QUIT CLEANING RIGHT NOW

1. **SNEAKERS.** Just buy dark-colored ones and wear them until they fall apart.

2. **GRILL GRATE.** When you're done grilling, leave the grill going. Close the cover over the grate and let any residue cook off for 15 minutes. Throw that wire brush away.

3. **SOCCER BALLS.** Everybody expects them to be marred and mud splotched. Think of it as a badge of honor.

4. **SHOWER CURTAIN LINER.** They're cheap. Throw your mildewed liner out and buy a new one every 6 months.

5. **PILLOW.** A washed pillow takes hours to dry. Throw it out and buy a new one every 6 to 8 months.

6. **STOVE DRIP PANS.** Use your grungy ones for everyday cooking, and keep a shiny new set to use when guests come.

7. **VENTILATION DUCTS.** Despite the advertising, regular professional duct cleaning is unnecessary.

8. **FIREPLACE WALLS.** Everybody expects a fireplace to have blackened walls. And you'll breathe even easier if you give up fires altogether.

9. **WAXING THE CAR.** The newer finishes are so tough cars don't need it anymore.

10. **MAKING THE BED.** Give it up—doctor's orders (see Chapter 6).

SPRING CLEANING: DON'T BE AN APRIL FOOL

Every spring you set aside two or three successive weekends on the calendar. You gather your cleaning armaments and warn your spouse that sudden out-of-town business trips will be viewed with deep suspicion. Then you tear through the house from attic to basement, a whirlwind of cleaning cloths, squirt bottles, brushes, and dusters.

If that doesn't sound like you, then at the very least you have the notion niggling at the back of your mind that you ought to perform spring cleaning every year. And you feel guilty about failing to.

If you feel good about doing a deep-down cleaning in your house once a year, go right ahead. But let's dispense with the guilt. The fact is, there is no reason for you to clean your house top to bottom all at once, and there is no reason to do this in the spring. The tradition of spring cleaning is a throwback to olden days when people shuttered their houses all winter and burned wood or coal for heat, spreading soot into every nook and cranny of the home. Come spring, those unfortunate souls couldn't wait to fling the windows open and start beating rugs, dusting lamps, and sweeping floors.

You don't have to do that—your heating system leaves the air clean. So free yourself of this dreaded ritual that wrecks your calendar or wracks you with guilt every April. A more reasonable approach: Manage the cleanliness of your home with a series of narrowly focused projects that are evenly distributed throughout the year.

every weekend? Furniture that's so fine you use it only for special occasions? A suit that's so delicate you're on tenterhooks every time you wear it? These possessions are Anxiety-Inducing Luxuries (AILments), and your own ego is making your life miserable. Gravitate toward modest, easy-care, functional possessions, even when you can afford the high-ticket stuff.

YOUR CHEATIN' HANDS

Now let's look at the rules of the game for cutting corners when you take that scrub brush in hand and actually attack some grime.

NARROW YOUR FOCUS With a schedule like yours, there's no time to clean the house from top to bottom. You'll get an appreciable amount of work done, however, if you attack mini cleaning projects throughout the week, 5 minutes here and 10 minutes there. This means taking a laser approach. You may not be able to clean the entire bathroom before you leave for work, but you *can* squirt cleaner on the tub and sponge it out.

BECOME A STORAGE NUT Make the best use of the storage in your home, and create new storage where none existed before. That's a key strategy to the easy elimination of clutter. This means mastering closets, shelving, boxes, bins, hooks, hangers, and more. Investment in storage gear pays off handsomely. See Chapter 3 for an in-depth discussion of clutter.

MAKE YOUR GEAR EASY TO GRAB The Accessibility Theorem goes like this: A cleaning task will be accomplished on a frequency that is inversely proportional to the distance between the object to be cleaned and the materials necessary to clean it. *Translation:* When it's hard to get to your cleaning tools, less cleaning gets done. At a minimum, keep a fully stocked cleaning station on each floor of the house.

ENGAGE THE BRAIN BEFORE CLEANING This is called the Thinking Wins Out (TWO) philosophy. Sure, it's tempting to let your mind wander while you're slogging through a cleaning chore. But the task will go more quickly and easily if you're ever alert for opportunities to cut corners: Set your plastic cutting board in the dishwasher rather than hand washing it; after brushing your teeth, touch up the mirror and several fixtures with one cleaning wipe; open your mail over a trash can and let all the junk fall into it. For every little labor-saving move you make, award yourself TWO points on your mental scoreboard.

BE WILLING TO REPLACE OLD GRUNGY ITEMS WITH FRESH NEW ONES Things like door mats, stovetop drip pans, shower curtains, and cookie sheets, for instance, are never really going to come clean. My advice is to run them into the ground, then replace them when they hit their inevitable irredeemably ragtag state.

A final note: I have no intention of becoming your new proverbial mother, looking over your shoulder as you clean. *You're* in charge. If you're not comfortable with instituting any particular piece of advice in this book, no problem—just slide on to the next item. Your mental health is more important than being a slave to someone else's ideas.

LET YOUR CLEANING TOOLS
DO THE WORK

The technology we use to clean our homes is always changing—sometimes ever so slowly, and sometimes in revolutionary ways. When we're right in the midst of them, the changes are difficult to appreciate. But look back to the beginning of the 20th century, when devices like the electric iron and the vacuum cleaner were first appearing in homes. Some folks were suspicious and even afraid of electrical devices. With booming industry drawing all of the servants away from household work, however, there was an enormous market for such cleaning "cheats."

The introduction of washing machines, dryers, easy-care fabrics, nonstick surfaces, self-cleaning ovens, and a nonstop parade of other labor-saving devices has had a radical effect on our lives. Cleaning tools are easy to take for granted as we slog through our daily chores, but the truth is that historically they have been one of the keys to human liberation. They have rescued us from the backbreaking, 24/7 task of managing a household. And the march of progress continues.

This brings up an intriguing question: What will be the next liberating device that historians will point to decades from now? Robotic vacuum cleaners? Windows that clean themselves? Automatic cat boxes? These gizmos—and scores of other innovative products—are available to you right now. You'll find them discussed in detail elsewhere in *How to Cheat at Cleaning*. The question is, Are you ready to incorporate such devices into your personal life?

Every individual has to answer that for himself or herself. Here's a quick set of questions to ask when you're considering adopting an innovative product. The BITE approach will help you decide whether to, uh, bite.

BETTER? Will this product actually perform the cleaning job better than my current method?

ILLUSION? Is there gimmickry involved? If it takes a half hour infomercial to sell this thing, could there be a reason it's not more popular?

TIME SAVING? Will this actually help me save time or cut corners?

ECONOMICAL? Is the extra convenience worth the cost of the item?

MANAGING YOUR TOOLS

If your only approach to cheating at cleaning is to not clean at all, well, you don't need a book to tell you how to find the hammock. But the savvy cheater-at-cleaning who wants to make the house presentable needs to know the best places to buy tools, the best ways to store them, and the best ways to put them into action. Here are some pointers.

BUYING

You will find the biggest selection of cleaning supplies, good prices, and brands you know at the big-box discount stores. So any time you can, buy your cleaning supplies there.

Janitorial supply stores are usually open to public, their prices are comparable to retail stores, and you can get larger containers of cleaners (often private labeled, but perfectly good). These stores are geared toward commercial cleaning people, however, and serving residential customers is not their priority.

At the supermarket, you might pay a little more and find less variety, but it's certainly convenient to buy an item or two during your regular grocery run.

STORING

Keep all of your cleaning tools in one spot in the house—a closet or in a corner of the laundry room, for instance—so you don't have to scramble all over the house looking

GREAT · GEAR

MICROFIBER: THE MIRACLE MATERIAL

Why are cleaning professionals ga-ga over microfiber cloths? Under the microscope, a conventional cotton fiber looks round—like a spaghetti noodle, says Tom Gustin, product manager for the Merry Maids[SM] cleaning service. It just pushes dirt along as you wipe. Microfibers are much finer and split into tiny wedge shapes that actually scoop up dirt and pull it into the fabric.

Here's a simple experiment that will demonstrate the remarkable difference in cleaning ability. Make two dots of peanut butter on your kitchen counter, a teaspoon each. Wipe up one dot with a cotton diaper—wipe, fold the diaper, and wipe again until the peanut butter is gone. You'll have to wipe three or four times. Wipe up the second dot with a microfiber cloth. You'll probably get it all on the first try.

Now rinse the diaper in warm water under the faucet and squeeze. That brown smear will remain until you launder the diaper. Rinse the microfiber cloth and squeeze. The microfiber cloth will come clean, ready for use again.

for gear when it's time to clean. This will save you time and increase the likelihood of actually getting some cleaning done. Within this storage area, cluster your products by their use—mop, bucket, and other floor-care stuff together; cloths, vacuum, and other dusting implements in another spot. If you have more than one kind of mop, hang them on a wall upside down so you can tell at

DISPOSABLES SWEEP THE MARKET

Among newly introduced products, Swiffer® is one of the biggest homeruns of the last decade. It's a quick-and-easy way to give a room that "somebody cares" feeling in a minimal amount of time.

There are lots of spin-off products—and competitors—but the core Swiffer apparatus is this: a permanent 46-inch mop handle with a 10-inch-wide mop head, plus disposable mopping pads (either wet or dry) that are easy to slap on and pull off. This cleaning approach lops a huge hassle out of the floor-cleaning process—namely, filling a bucket, pouring in cleaner, hauling it around, dipping and squeezing out your mop, and pouring the water out at the end.

Disposable mop heads will snatch up dust and small particles, but they won't handle chunkier stuff like dead leaves from your houseplants, tracked in pine needles, or bits of dry pet food. You can, of course, use the mop to corral this stuff into one area and then get it up later with a brush and dustpan. At a certain point, the mop head will get overloaded with dirt (in my house, anyway) and lose its grabbing power. Stand over a trash can and pick off some of the debris with your fingers to get a little more mileage out of the pad. Also, you can flip the cloth over and use the other side.

Once in a while, when you've just put on a clean, dry cloth, use it to quickly wipe down the walls of the room. (Besides painting every several years, this is the only way that walls in my house get cleaned.) You can use the edge of the mop head to dust the tops of door frames, too.

a glance which is which, says Cynthia Braun, a professional organizer in Lake Grove, New York. Also, cluster all of your refill bottles in one spot and, at the end of each cleaning session, top off any bottles that you used.

If you have a second floor, keep a second cleaning station up there, fully stocked with everything you need to maintain the upstairs rooms.

USING

The best corner-cutting house-cleaners know that you need some kind of device for moving several cleaning items around the house with you as you work. This technique saves you from making multiple trips back to the cleaning closet. For most people, a tote tray is the way to go—a rectangular caddy with a raised handle and pocket-like bins all around it for holding squirt bottles, the whisk broom, cloths, and such. If you don't have a caddy, a plastic bucket will do in a pinch.

If you really want to show off your cheat-at-cleaning credentials, Braun recommends buying a tool belt at your home-improvement store. You can hang your most commonly used cleaning implements off the belt and you won't even have to bend over to reach for your caddy. When you're not wearing the belt, just hang it around the caddy handle.

THE BASIC CHECKLIST

I asked Tom Gustin, product manager for the Merry Maids cleaning service based in Memphis, Tennessee, to help compile a list of the most basic cleaning tools that any cheat-at-cleaning enthusiast would want to have in his or her closet. Aside from specialized tasks such as polishing silver, the following tools will handle virtually any household cleaning duty:

SCRUBBER SPONGE These are the household sponges that have an abrasive surface on one side for scouring tough grime. Scrubber sponges are color coded. Look for the kind with a white scrubber pad, meaning it's the least abrasive and least likely to scratch surfaces. "I would have two—one that you use for bathrooms and one that you use for kitchens and everywhere else," Gustin says.

TOILET BRUSH Yup, the wand that goes where others fear to tread. The all-plastic kind won't scratch the porcelain, whereas those with a wire center can. Make sure it comes with a little bowl-like stand that will catch drips when you're done. If you think *yuck* every time you see a toilet brush, switch to the super-convenient disposable variety.

VACUUM CLEANERS The hardcore cheater uses two vacuum cleaners, Gustin says—one conventional vacuum cleaner and one handheld vac. (Indoors, stick to the plug-in kind, since the recharging systems on some cordless models can be unreliable.) Use the big vacuum for broad floor cleaning and the handheld with its extension for cleaning corners, cobwebs, and tight spaces. With this one-two punch, you'll never need a broom. Gustin prefers the conventional upright vacuum cleaner to the canister or backpack styles. Look for a handheld that offers disposable paper dust bags as an option for easy, mess-free changes. If you can spare the expense, put a conventional vacuum cleaner on each floor so you won't have to haul it up and down the stairs. Use extension cords on your vacuum cleaners so you don't have to find a new electrical outlet every few minutes.

DUSTER Gustin likes lambs-wool dusters that come with an extension wand—they're great for dusting the tops of doors and the blades of ceiling fans. A good alternative: Fluffy, disposable dusting heads that fit onto an extension wand.

MOP Pass up the string mops, forge on past the sponge mops, and head straight for a flat mop. This device is good for wet or dry mopping and has a removable mopping pad that you can toss into the washing machine. They don't require wringing out and can reach under furniture more easily than conventional mops. Or jump whole-hog into one of the disposable mop systems—you just throw away the mopping pad when you're done.

BUCKET You'll need an all-purpose container for hauling liquids for cleaning windows, cars, floors, and more. Gustin uses a conventional round, 10-quart model.

BROOM Gustin actually never uses a broom, but you'll need one if you didn't run out and buy a handheld vacuum like he told you to.

CLEANING CLOTHS Microfiber cleaning cloths are superior at grabbing up dirt. Acceptable alternatives are cloth diapers or surgical "huck" towels.

CLEANERS At the very least, you'll want each of these:

* ☀ Disinfecting cleaner for sanitizing
* ☀ All-purpose cleaner
* ☀ Glass cleaner
* ☀ Toilet bowl cleaner
* ☀ Floor cleaner

> ## DISPOSABLE WIPES: TOSSING OUT A NEW STRATEGY

A few decades ago, disposable cleaning wipes had one lowly function: cleaning babies' bottoms. Baby wipes made perfect sense. Laundering anything that's covered in poop is pretty unappealing. Disposable diapers were a hit, after all, so why not wipes?

Then product researchers discovered that parents were cheating. They were using baby wipes for unauthorized purposes—say, wiping sticky fingers, doing touch-up cleaning in the bathroom, or blotting up stains on the couch. "Whoa," cried the ever-attentive product researchers, "maybe we ought to create a full range of disposable wipes for lots of different uses!"

So household-cleaning wipes emerged in the 1990s. Then dry, electrostatic wipes and cloths burst upon the scene in 1999, and the disposable wipe market has been expanding steadily ever since.

WARY OF WIPES?

Not all consumers have bought into the idea of disposable wipes. More than a third of all Americans have never tried any kind of disposable wipe, according to a survey done by the Soap and Detergent Association. That's too bad, because they offer enormous benefits:

* **Super convenience.** Everything you need is right there in one compact package—the cleaning cloth plus the cleaning chemical you need, all premeasured.

* **Portability.** Wipes usually come in convenient, resealable packaging that fits easily into a purse, glove box, desk drawer, gym bag, suitcase, or picnic basket. They're perfect for people on the go.

* **No mess.** There are no cleaning tools to wash or put away after the job is done. Just toss the wipe in the trash.

* **Tough on germs.** Whatever germs aren't killed outright by the wipes are just tossed into the trash can. They don't linger on your sponge or cleaning cloth, only to get spread around your home again.

* **Versatility.** While some wipes have narrow, specific purposes—everything from spiffing up your jewelry to cleaning blinds—many are good for a wide variety of cleaning tasks.

* **Reasonable cost.** Wipe users surveyed say the convenience definitely outweighs the expense.

So if you've been reluctant to plunge into the world of disposable wipes, you're in for an eye-popping surprise. Your cleaning chores are profoundly more tedious than they need to be. "I think you could probably clean your whole house using wipes," says Janet Nelson, a Ross, Iowa–based spokesperson for The Maids Home Services[SM].

Disposable wipes are easy to find—they're now a staple in supermarkets, discount stores, and home-improvement stores. They're incredibly easy to use as well, but there's one rule that too many people ignore, says Brian Sansoni, vice president of the Soap and Detergent Association: Read the package label first. You'll find any safety warnings on the label. Also, you'll find out what your wipes can and can't do. Not all kill germs, for instance, not all can be flushed down the toilet, and some (such as furniture polish wipes) shouldn't be used on floors because they'll make them slippery.

You may be concerned that disposable wipes aren't environmentally friendly. They don't actually amount to a lot of refuse, however—less than five hundredths of 1 percent of solid household waste, whereas newspapers and plastic make up 10 percent. Also, some brands have started making their packaging from recyclable materials.

Read on for specific advice on how to get the most out of disposable wipes around the home and when you're out and about.

WIPE OUT HOURS OF LABOR

Use disinfecting wipes on food preparation surfaces and utensils to protect your family from bacteria that can cause serious illness. Check the packaging to make sure that the wipes you're using will kill germs. Carefully follow the label's instructions for disinfecting, too. You'll probably be told to wipe the surface down and let it air dry for 10 minutes. Then you may need to wipe again with a wet paper towel to remove chemical residue.

Remember that not all wipes are intended for all purposes. If your wipes promise to disinfect hard surfaces, they may be too harsh to use for hand washing or wiping baby bottoms, for instance.

TUNE UP THE BATHROOM In Chapter 5, we discuss how to clean your bathroom in 7 minutes (12 minutes for the deluxe job). If even that seems like too much slave duty in the throne room, you can double or triple the amount of time between cleanings with the use of disposable wipes. Just perform this easy, 1-minute routine twice a week:

Take an all-purpose or glass-cleaner wipe and clean the mirror and the window, then use it to pick up any accumulated dust or grime around the top of the tub, the top edge of the tile and, last, the base of the toilet. Toss the wipe out. Now take a disinfecting wipe and clean the faucet, the countertop, the toilet handle, and the toilet seat. Toss it. Take another disinfecting wipe and run it across the top rim of the tub, the sides, and across the drain to pick up any hair. Done!

STOP DIRT AT THE DOOR Stash a package of general-purpose wipes near any door where kids and pets come and go, suggests Joni Hilton, creator of Holy Cow™ cleaning products in Sacramento, California. Hilton says she keeps wipes near the back door, particularly in the summer. When kids come in from playing, grimy shoes and hands get a wipe down.

BREAK THE SPONGE HABIT Disposable dishwashing wipes could put a barrier between your family and disease. Unfortunately, the sponges that often are used for dishwashing can collect food particles down in their dark, moist recesses. "They're a germ factory," says Sansoni. Disposable dishwashing wipes will change that. They come already filled with dishwashing detergent and have a soft side and an abrasive side for scrubbing. You can use them a couple of times, Sansoni says, and just throw them out.

SECRET INGREDIENT: ALCOHOL Keep alcohol-based wipes in the kitchen. Not only does the alcohol kill germs but it cuts grease, too. These wipes will make quick work of the stovetop and those grubby stove knobs, for instance.

THINK BIG Many disposable wipes are tiny things—smaller than a standard washcloth, Nelson notes. Many cleaning jobs around the house—like wiping down an entire toilet—will require two or three wipes. To make your life even easier, keep an eye out for the larger, thicker wipes, which pick up more grime without

MESSY DOGS? FETCH A WIPE

A pet expert based in New York City, Charlotte Reed, shares her two-bedroom apartment with a parrot, 13 finches, two Persian cats and three dogs. She uses disinfecting wipes daily on counters where she prepares food, on the floor around the pet-food bowls, around the litter boxes, and under the 67-inch-high birdcage.

She keeps her pets away from newly wiped areas until they've aired out, so they aren't exposed to the disinfecting chemicals. She's also reluctant to use harsh cleaners around her birds, so for cleaning around her feathered friends she uses mild antibacterial hand wipes.

Since the dogs romp around outside frequently, they're particularly wipe intensive. When they come in, Reed uses little puppy gates to confine them to the kitchen until they've been cleaned up. General-purpose wipes work well on their paws. It's particularly important to wipe their feet in the winter, she says, because sidewalk salt will irritate their paws if it's not removed.

requiring frequent changes. You can often find these in the diaper section of your supermarket.

KEEP THEM UNDER WRAPS Most wipes come in a resealable container that will keep them from drying out. But if a package you've opened is going to be sitting around for several weeks, pop it into a zip-closing plastic bag for extra protection.

KEEP BUGS AT BAY Viruses that cause colds and flu can live on surfaces around your home for as long as 72 hours. So if someone in your home is sniffling and sneezing, regularly disinfect any commonly touched surfaces. This will reduce the chance of that infection getting passed along. Check the label on your wipes to make sure they'll kill cold and flu viruses. Wipe down appliances (don't forget the refrigerator handle and the microwave touch pad), counters, tables, cabinet handles, doorknobs, light switches, telephones, television controls, remotes, and video game controllers.

SEND WIPES TO SCHOOL One in five parents say their kids' schools lack the proper personal hygiene products needed to prevent illness. So why not take a proactive role with your child? Slip a hand wipe into her lunch box each day and instruct her to clean her hands before she eats. Put it in a plastic bag to prevent drying, or use the kind that comes individually packaged.

Germ-killing wipes, disposable mop heads, miracle fabrics—the space program may be attention grabbing, but science affects you much more directly in the cleaning closet. When you become a fan of innovative cleaning products, your chores become negligible and white space opens up on your calendar—free time for more important things. Less work. More fun. That's what cheating is all about.

CLUTTER CONTROL
MADE EASY

If eliminating the clutter in your home sounds like a lot of work, consider how much work co-existing with that clutter *causes*. Professional organizers say if your home weren't cluttered, 40 percent of your housework would evaporate. Also, if your office is orderly, you save yourself *weeks* of time each year—time that's typically spent looking for papers and other materials. Yup, de-cluttering your home is itself a way to cheat at cleaning: It requires less effort than not de-cluttering.

Now, stop groaning—nobody's going to tell you to get your home ready for a *House Beautiful*® photo shoot. That kind of "perfection" is no more real world than a Hollywood back lot. More reasonable goals leave room for the occasional messy dresser top, jumbled car trunk, or chaotic pantry shelf, goals such as:

- ❋ Being able to find possessions when they're needed.

- ❋ Having a home you're comfortable showing to friends and colleagues.

- ❋ Having a place in your home for every possession and a simple, ongoing process to get it there.

THE CLUTTER-BUSTER'S PLEDGE

1.

Every possession has to earn its keep.
It must have a function in my daily life.

2.

Every possession will have a home.
No more setting things down "just for now."

3.

I will not measure my personal value by my possessions.

4.

Sentimentality is a home wrecker.
I will use it sparingly when deciding what items to
keep and what items to dispose of.

5.

De-cluttering is an ongoing lifestyle,
not a finite project.

6.

Absolutely everything I own will, at some time,
become of no use to me.

7.

No one, not even my kids, will ever establish
a museum devoted to my worldly goods.

In this chapter, we'll look first at the "mental" side of clutter busting—simple ways of thinking about clutter that will help your home automatically fall into order. Then we'll tackle the physical aspects of clutter: working with containers, shelving, and other hardware and getting optimum use out of the storage spaces available to you. Naturally, this chapter is brimming with the world's best big-impact-for-minimal-work, corner-cutting advice.

THE INS AND OUTS OF CLUTTER

Imagine a child's toy box. Once a month, the child gets one new toy and puts it into the box. Every 6 months, the child stops playing with one of these toys— it's either broken or he finally admits that he's outgrown it, and he gets rid of it. What's going to happen over time, with more toys going into the box than are coming out? The toy box will overflow into an unsightly mess, and the child won't be able to find the toys he wants.

Your house is much like that. Most of us have many more possessions entering the house (new stuff) than we have exiting the house (worn-out stuff). It doesn't take a math genius to realize that this will eventually overburden all storage systems in even the largest homes. Possessions will be spilling out onto the floor, swamping the counters, and stacking to the ceiling in the garage. It's clutter.

Why does this happen? In broad terms, we are the beneficiaries of the Industrial Revolution. Never in the history of humans have so many goods been available for so little money. Just to make sure that we remain suitably wanton in grabbing up new possessions, a mammoth marketing machine eggs us on with hundreds of "buy" messages every day. This explosion of consumer goods is so recent, historically speaking, that society hasn't developed strong enough defenses against the onslaught. After all, there's very little money to be found by providing the more helpful kinds of messages, such as "Purge your possessions and live more simply" or "You don't really need a third television." So businesses don't do that. As a matter of self-preservation, you're going to have to reinforce the "buy-less" lifestyle all on your own.

Start with "The Clutter-Buster's Pledge" on p. 24. These seven simple commitments will help you curtail your hyper-buying ways, break your irrational emotional bond with possessions, and manage the stuff you do keep so that you have the kind of home environment you really want. Photocopy the pledge, tape it to the inside of your closet door, and review it before every shopping trip. If a mere "attitude adjustment" can slay the Clutter Monster once and for all—well, that's the very best kind of cleaning cheat.

STEP UP THE OUTFLOW

As you stem the flow of goods into your house, of course, your clutter problems will become easier to manage. However, there's a second part of the equation on which you also can have a major effect: the flow of goods out of your house. Here are some easy ways to improve your home's "outflow"—above and beyond taking the trash out each week.

QUESTION YOUR POSSESSIONS When you're de-cluttering and you're not sure whether you want to keep an item, ask yourself these five questions, says Kerul Kassel, a productivity consultant in Saint Cloud, Florida:

1. When did I last use this? If you haven't used it for 6 months to a year, get rid of it. (Seasonal items are an exception.)

2. Will I be able to find this again? This applies in particular to papers. If the item doesn't have a proper "home" where you'll be able to find it again, you might as well toss it.

3. What shape will this be in when I retrieve it? Aging computer equipment will be useless in a jiffy. The same goes for fashion items and food.

4. Is it costing me more to store this, on the off chance that I may need it some day, than it would for me to borrow or buy it in the future? Think in terms of space in the home and the mental burden of dealing with the item: Do you want to be caretaker of this thing for the next 5 years to 10 years?

5. Is owning this thing *truly* improving the overall quality of my life?

CLUSTER THOSE OUTBOUND ITEMS Create a little "way station" in your home for items that you've decided are headed out the door, says C. Lee Cawley, a professional organizer in

6 INDICATIONS THAT IT'S JUNK

Can't decide whether that 80-pound concrete gargoyle is junk or a treasure? Lindsay Peroff, of the clutter-removal company 1-800-GOT-JUNK?℠, says the following factors indicate that an item is junk:

1. You can't remember the last time you used it.
2. There's a layer of dust on it.
3. It's broken.
4. It's out of date.
5. You can't remember why you saved it.
6. You just don't want it in your home any more.

WHY WAIT UNTIL YOU DIE?

New York City architect Evan Galen has an interesting strategy for helping you sort through possessions that clutter your home. "Imagine that you've died and your family is coming around to look at your stuff and deal with it," he says. "Whatever they would keep that you don't especially need, give it to them *now*."

If you have an item that your family would not want—and you don't want it either—get rid of it now, he says.

Alexandria, Virginia. These could include items you're donating to a thrift store, a tool you borrowed from a neighbor, rental videos, library books, dry-cleaning, and clothing you need to return to a department store. If these things are lying all about the house, you won't remember to take them with you the next time you're running errands— they'll be that much more clutter. If they're all assembled near the door, you'll remember to snatch them up on your way out. Cawley likes to hang a shoe bag–like organizer on the back of her door. You also could hang an organizer on the back of your coat closet door or put the items in shopping bags on the floor of the coat closet.

GET ON A CHARITY'S PHONE LIST Many organizations regularly pick up donated items from residences. Phone around to find the groups that will call you the day before they plan to have a truck in your neighborhood. Make sure you have a clear idea of what kind of items the charity accepts. Some won't take furniture, for instance.

SELL YOUR CLUTTER TO OTHERS Make a yearly yard sale an institution in your home. Don't just scramble around the day before a yard sale, looking for disposable items in your house. All year long, sock items away in boxes in the corner of your basement—items of obvious value that nevertheless have no place in your life. Three months before the day of your yard sale, distribute a flier among your neighbors, asking them to schedule their yard sales on the same day. Have them share the cost of a classified ad in the newspaper on the day of the sale—bargain hunters from miles around will be attracted to a street with multiple yard sales. Call around to find a charity that will agree to pick up all of the leftover items from you and your neighbors on the day after the sale. And make this a personal rule: No yard sale item may come back into the house.

HIRE A PRO TO TAKE IT AWAY

It's a sign of our times that businesses such as 1-800-GOT-JUNK?^{SM} are thriving. "We find the main reason we're growing is that people are spending money storing junk they're never going to use," says Lindsay Peroff, a representative of the company based in Vancouver, British Columbia. Her company will send employees to your home to pick up any clutter you ask them to. This saves you from having to load the junk, truck it away, and arrange for dumping—the company takes care of it all. Their services are particularly advantageous if you're overwhelmed by a mountain of possessions you just want out of your life. Peroff says an average job costs $260 and fills half of a truck the size of a Federal Express^{SM} delivery vehicle. The company has 200 locations in North America, covering most large cities and their suburbs. There's probably a branch—or a similar company—near you.

ONE MAN'S JUNK . . .

You see some strange sights when it's your job to remove clutter from other people's homes and businesses. Lindsay Peroff, of the clutter-removal company 1-800-GOT-JUNK?, says the following items are among the more peculiar unwanted possessions they have hauled away for clients. (They make sure the owner is aware of the value of any item.)

• Prosthetic legs

• 18,000 cans of sardines

• 13 huge porcelain Buddha statues

• 19,000 pounds of frozen animal carcasses

• Antique rifles

• A defused bomb from World War I.

• An antique silver set.

• A 1954 Martin® guitar. (The owner said, "Do whatever you want to with it." It sold for more than $8,000 on eBay®.)

• Half a truckload of expired dog food.

A junk-removal crew also came across a totally unexpected item hidden amid one resident's clutter: an engagement ring that had been missing for 30 years. *That* was returned to the grateful owner.

ORGANIZE BY STATIONS

Trying to de-clutter a typical home is enough to make anyone hyperventilate. However, Kassel has a deliciously easy trick for organizing any home—a technique that strikes at the heart of clutter: View your home as a collection of "stations" for performing the household's various functions.

Let's consider an obvious example: Food preparation is a core function of the home, and the station for that is invariably the kitchen. You probably do an adequate job of ensuring that all items you need for food preparation are quickly and easily found right there in the kitchen—not in the basement, not in the garage, and not under little Joey's bed. As you stand in your primary food-fixing spot, the items you need most—cutting board, knives, and frying pan, for instance—should be right at your fingertips. Infrequently used items should have homes farther away—your monster-size soup pot might go on a high shelf in the pantry, for example.

How does the idea of stations in the home control clutter? Well, in a home organized by function, items naturally gravitate toward where they need to be. The "home" for each item becomes more readily apparent, and an out-of-place or nonfunctional item will stand out like a streaker in the village square. If an object in your home is not serving any purpose, you have to ask yourself why it's there—and set it on a fast track out the door. (Okay, you might argue that art objects aren't part of a "station," but your display items do serve a purpose and need to be managed as a group.) Also, the stations concept performs the psychological trick of breaking your home down into smaller, easily managed compartments. You may not be able to de-clutter the entire house when you find a spare 10 minutes, but you can do wonders with your sewing area in that amount of time.

When you regard your home in terms of stations, an interesting strategy emerges that will save you a lot of time and bother: Every

THE ABCs OF CDs

Stop alphabetizing your CDs—right now. If you have all of your music neatly arranged from Abba to Zappa, you have to reorganize them every time you bring home a new CD. Instead, professional organizer C. Lee Cawley recommends that you organize your music by broad categories such as "Classic Rock," " '80s New Wave," "Jazz," and "Party Music." For each category, leave 20 percent of the space open to accommodate growth. That way, you don't have to move all of your CDs around each time you buy a new disk. Also, you don't have to return a disk to one precise slot on the shelf—anywhere on the shelf will do, as long as it's in the correct broad category.

"It's all about retrieval," Cawley says. That is, don't arrange your collection according to how you want to put CDs *away;* arrange it according to where you will look for the CDs when you want them. Besides, who do you think you are? A librarian?

If space is at a premium in your entertainment area, here's a supercompact way to store your CDs and DVDs: Throw out all of the plastic cases for your disks. Buy binders filled with the special sleeves made just for CDs, and slide each of your disks into these pockets. Tossing out the cases may feel radical at first, but it's liberating once you get used to it. The binders keep all of your disks together, make them easy to browse, keep them clean, and take up much less space on a shelf. If you're willing to put a tad more work into this system, pull any liner notes out of the CD cases and tuck them into a pocket of the binder. For DVDs, photocopy the case, hole punch the paper, and clip it into the rings of the binder.

station deserves to be completely outfitted with the tools and materials necessary to perform the assigned function. This will save you enormous amounts of time walking about the house looking for the myriad objects you need, say, to prepare a package for mailing. Your mail station will have tape, envelopes, boxes, stamps, scissors, labels, and anything else you need to get a package ready. No trekking to the kitchen or sewing room for scissors. The extra expense for duplicate supplies is nominal (those supplies *will* get used, after all) and the payoff is huge.

Here are quick notes about just a few other stations you might have in your home. Depending on your lifestyle, you'll likely want to invent some of your own:

WORK STATION. Everything you need for conducting business, managing finances, and corresponding. See Chapter 8 for more on home offices.

OVERRUN BY BOXES?

Every time you buy a small appliance, you read the following instructions in the manual: "Save all packaging material in case you need to return this appliance to the manufacturer." So now 500 cubic feet of empty cardboard boxes have overrun your basement.

To heck with that—throw those boxes away. In the unlikely event that you need to ship an appliance, just take it to one of those private mailing stores. They're experts at safely packing up any kind of delicate object you can imagine. Simply plop the bare appliance on the counter and give the clerk the shipping address and phone number.

CLEANING STATION. Stock a portable cleaning caddy with spray cleaners, dusting cloths, brushes, and wipes. Have a cleaning station on each floor of the house.

LAUNDRY STATION. This contains everything you need for clothing management—washer, dryer, detergent, stain remedies, and iron and ironing board (if you must). You need a bar for hanging garments and good light for inspecting clothes for stains.

FITNESS STATION. A welcoming place with plenty of room for your treadmill, stationary bike, and weights, plus easy access to any audio or video gear you need.

AUTOMOTIVE STATION. Typically in the garage, carport, or shed, it contains car-cleaning materials, auto tools, extra windshield fluid, oil, and coolant.

CRAFT OR HOBBY STATION. Put all of your craft or hobby tools, materials, and reference books in one place, organized in easy-access storage containers. Consider such needs as good lighting, a work surface, and ventilation.

TOOL STATION. An unused wall in the basement is ideal for a large pegboard or some other wall-mounted tool-organizing system. Have a worktable nearby, plus small grab-and-go toolkits already outfitted for your most common jobs. You need plenty of small containers for sorting hardware.

ENTERTAINMENT STATION. Cabinets for television, sound system, electronic game systems, plus generous storage for CDs, DVDs, game controllers, remote controls, and headphones.

DESIGN DIRT AWAY

AN OFF-THE-WALL STORAGE IDEA

To add an enormous amount of storage space—and therefore reduce clutter—in even a tiny home, why not build a hidden, shallow closet that runs the entire width of one wall? This works in any room—and even in a corridor, says New York City architect Evan Galen.

Galen likes to build these wall-size closets from floor to ceiling, on invisible hinges and then paints or wallpapers them to look like other walls in the room. They take only 8 inches of space out of a room, but they can hide plenty of shelves, hanging clothes, cleaning gear, and more.

GIFT-WRAPPING STATION. This is the spot for all your wrapping paper, ribbon, tape, scissors, gift tags, plus a broad work surface. You might want to combine this with a mailing station.

Cawley recommends one more kind of station in the home: Each person in the house should have a personal staging area or launch pad. This is an assigned, dedicated spot where that person can park her purse, briefcase, cell phone, PDA, and keys. When she goes out into the world, all of the objects she needs to take along are right there. When she comes home at night, she drops everything in the same place. Kids need launch pads, too, Crawley says, for their book bags and shoes. The launch pad might be a drawer near the door, a bin, a basket, a shelf, or part of a counter.

SIMPLE STEPS FOR ATTACKING CLUTTER

No one is immune to clutter. As carefully as you might train yourself and your family to stop clutter before it starts, little infestations are inevitable now and then—a mound of magazines and books on the coffee table, Lego® pieces and action figures spilling across the family room floor, a car trunk brimming with tennis equipment and broken umbrellas. That's only natural. But you can make a clutter-busting lifestyle just as natural with these simple steps, which were partially inspired by Courtney Shaver, a representative of The Container Store®, based in Coppell, Texas.

1. **NARROW YOUR FOCUS.** Which are you more likely to accomplish over the next month: A 5-hour de-cluttering session, going top-to-bottom in your house? Or five separate 1-hour de-cluttering sessions, hitting one clutter hot spot at a time? The latter, of course. If you wait until you can tackle the entire house, you'll never get around to it. Make a habit of launching 1-hour clutter attacks once or twice a week. Having that one corner of your home gleaming with order will inspire you to start plotting your next attack on clutter.

2. **PULL AND PURGE.** Drag everything out of the area that you're de-cluttering. If your target is a pantry shelf, for instance, take all of the cans, boxes, kitchen gizmos, paper towel rolls, and jugs of juice off the shelf and spread them out on the floor. Be ruthless about disposing of anything you don't need, has expired, or otherwise has no function in your life.

3. **CLEAN.** You won't see your pantry this empty for months or years to come, so vacuum and dust it thoroughly. Some of the items you're saving could stand a wipe down, too.

4. **CATEGORIZE.** Cluster all the like things together. In the pantry example, you would put the pasta and canned spaghetti sauce together, the soups and stock together, the baking ingredients together, the snack foods together, and the paper goods together.

5. **SET PRIORITIES.** Decide what items you need easiest access to (they'll go on the mid-level shelves) and what items are used less often (high shelves, low shelves, and remote nooks).

6. **CONTAIN.** Decide how best to display and contain your items (use bins, baskets, hooks, and mini-shelves, for instance). Your arrangement should make the best use of

the space available. Items should be visible and accessible. Use a flexible storage system that can adapt to changing needs.

| **STRATEGIC STORAGE** |

A 10-year-old I know very well had two bookshelves in his bedroom that were chock-full of books he wasn't using—most of them meant for younger kids. The rest of his room was a mess because he was out of storage space. Hoping to create more storage for him, I asked him to pull off the shelves all the books he was willing to sell in the next yard sale. He pulled out 25 slim volumes. Disappointed, I then asked him to remove all of the books he was willing to put into storage in the crawl space. He filled several boxes with 400 books!

The moral of the story: Storage space is an important psychological tool. One reason homes stay cluttered is a reluctance to part with possessions. Putting them into storage is a comfortable alternative. When these items have been out of sight for a year, it will be easier emotionally to give them away or sell them.

Storage is a sort of magic wand for creating an orderly house. This applies not only to items you want to stash away for the long term but also to items you want to keep orderly—but still accessible—for daily use. Let's take a look at how to best manage the storage spaces you have and how you can easily create new storage space when you need more.

WORKING WITH CONTAINERS

Give yourself permission to go crazy with containers. They're one of the most basic tools for home organization, and they're usually inexpensive. Here are some ideas for working with containers, from professional organizers and The Container Store.

USE TRANSPARENT CONTAINERS If you have items stored in opaque, unlabeled containers, you're going to forget what's in there. Those objects may be out of your way, but retrieving them will be a hassle. So make sure any storage containers you use are either see-through or labeled.

STACK THOSE BINS Vertical space in the typical home is woefully neglected. Stacking bins in your office, entertainment area, pantry, bedroom, or craft room will add tons of storage while only occupying a few square feet of floor space. For convenience, look for bins with slide-out drawers on the side.

TURN STACKS ON THEIR SIDE If you have a spot in your house where papers collect—say, on a dresser, counter, table, or credenza—professional organizer C. Lee Cawley says you can bring them to order with a snap of the fingers. All you have to do is turn the pile onto its side. Buy a vertical folder organizer from an office store and plop it in the same spot where those papers gather. Create a folder for each category of paper and sort the documents into the files. The papers take up no more space, yet they're instantly retrievable and look better to boot.

PUT SUPPLIES ON WHEELS Rolling carts are a powerful storage strategy, particularly for supplies that you need access to only for temporary work periods. Roll the cart out while you're working, then roll it back to a closet or a remote corner of the room when you're done. This works particularly well for cooking, office supplies, shop tools, and arts and crafts.

COVER THE CARDBOARD Alexandria Lighty, owner of the House Doctors Handyman Service^{SM}, likes storage boxes that blend in with the decor of the room where they're used. This is neither difficult nor expensive to achieve. Drop by an office-supply store and pick up a set of corrugated cardboard boxes, the handled kind meant for holding office files. Spritz the exterior of each box with spray glue and cover them in a fabric that works well with the rest of the room. For instance, you could cover the boxes in the same material you used for the room's curtains. Park these boxes on a shelf. When it's time to straighten up the room, pull the boxes out, dump the out-of-place objects into them, and slide them home again.

A LITTLE HELP FROM YOUR FURNITURE

Lighty likes to outfit her rooms with furniture that's designed to keep clutter off the floor and out of sight. Here are some of her favorites:

ARMOIRES. Lighty has stationed one of these closet-like cabinets in her living room, her dining room, and in each bedroom. In the main living areas, her armoires house the televisions, game systems, and related gear. They're smaller and less imposing than the typical entertainment center, and she can change the tone of the room just by closing the door to hide the TV. In the children's bedrooms, armoires provide a compact hanging space that's easy for kids to manage themselves.

FOYER CREDENZAS. Many homes have some kind of surface near the front door where people coming in drop their purses, hats, keys, and such. Why not use a long dresser, one with six to nine drawers, and assign a drawer to each member of the household? That way the miscellaneous personal items will be hidden—but also easy to find when each person dashes out the door for the day.

STORAGE BENCHES. Shop for the kind of bench that doubles as a storage box, and park it in the foyer or in the mudroom. Your children can toss their book bags in there when they get home from school. Little tykes will love stashing a jacket, hat, and gloves there, since they usually can't reach such items in a conventional closet. If you ask arriving guests to remove their shoes, a bench-box near the door hides the pile of footwear better than the commonly used basket.

DAY BEDS. Unlike sofas, day beds are built high enough that storage bins can be stashed underneath. With a few pillows across the back, you have a comfortable seating area, plus a backup bed for overnight guests. Use a bed skirt to hide the bins below.

MANAGING YOUR STORAGE ROOMS

When you have a bulky object you need to store away, where ya gonna turn? To the garage, attic, basement, crawl space, or shed, of course. These spaces are the utility infielders of the home front, the locations of choice for yard tools, shop tools, bicycles, out-of-season clothes, food bought in bulk, rarely used kitchen gear, backup refrigerators, sports equipment, and much more. Because they house such a hodgepodge of possessions, they stretch your organizational skills to the limit. With a few savvy techniques, however, you can vanquish those cluttered obstacle courses that build up in

GREAT·GEAR

CRAWL-SPACE HELPERS

A storage area that is impractical, inaccessible, or uncomfortable to reach will rarely be used. The traditional crawl space presents a number of challenges to the homeowner. Because of the low ceiling, you have to scrape and bruise your knees while you move storage items around. You can't stand straight up, of course, so moving heavy boxes more that a yard or two is a Herculean feat. And because crawl spaces are often damp, you risk starting up a mold farm on your stored goods. The following items, available at any home-improvement store, should be standard gear for any crawl space:

- **KNEE PADS AND WORK GLOVES.** These will protect your hands and knees as you crawl about on the concrete. Store them permanently on a hook or shelf right at the entrance to your crawl space.

- **DOLLY.** A flat, four-wheeled dolly makes it easy to whisk heavy objects from one side of the crawl space to another. Tie a rope to the dolly so you can sit still and pull objects toward you.

- **DEHUMIDIFIER.** Installing a dehumidifier in your crawl space will help to keep moisture and mold at bay. So you don't have to empty water from the dehumidifier manually, run a hose from its collection bin to a drain.

your storage rooms. Who knows—you might actually be able to park your car in your garage again.

Here's how to get optimum, organized use out of your storage rooms with the least amount of effort, according Lighty and her colleagues at House Doctors Handyman Service:

* Cover the perimeter of the room in wire shelving, pegboard, hooks, and similar storage. With this single measure, you will triple your home's storage capacity. Wire shelves and pegboard are sturdy, don't hold dust, and don't require painting, so upkeep on them is zero.

* Use heavy-duty hooks mounted on overhead beams to hang such bulky items as hoses, extension cords, and bicycles. If you have open beams, look for the easy-mount style that will slip right over the beam, or grasp the beam, and hang down. If the beams are covered by drywall, use screw-in hooks.

* Use tall laundry hampers and garbage bins (you'll clean them first, right?) to hold basketballs, hockey sticks, football pads, helmets, and other bulky athletic equipment.

* Suspend a shelf from the ceiling to hold long, flat items such as skis, snowboards, and canoe paddles.

* An old golf bag makes a great holder for long-handled tools such as hoes, rakes, and tree pruners.

* Allow each family member to hang no more than two coats in the main coat closet. Other coats can be stored in each person's private closet, and they can be rotated seasonally. This way, there's plenty of hanging space for guests in the main closet. Also, people will be more likely to hang their coats—instead of dropping them on the furniture—if it's easy to find a spot in the closet.

HUNT DOWN NEW STORAGE SPACE

Gather up a pen, a memo pad, and a measuring tape. Take a 20-minute tour of your house, from your attic to your basement, from the garage to the shed. Jot down notes about every space in your home that could conceivably be turned into storage. Note the location of each space and its measurements. Include in your list the following:

* Open walls where racks, shelving, or organizers could be installed.

* Odd gaps that remain from the building's design— for instance, the space under stairways or open area above cabinets.

* The backs of doors, where you could install hooks, racks, or organizers.

QUIT WAITING FOR PERMISSION

Tired of arguing with family members who get absurdly attached to items cluttering your house—your husband's 3-year-old hunting catalogs, for instance, or little Jeanie's 17 Popsicle®-stick creations on the kitchen counter?

Well, think about it: Nobody's really keeping track of each and every one of those items. Occasionally pick out one innocuous item and toss it out without asking permission. Bury it deep in the kitchen trash can, or toss it in there just as you're taking out the garbage. If, by some astounding chance, someone realizes it's missing 6 months later, you can just shrug your shoulders and say you haven't seen it lately. This falls into the "little white lie" category. That's okay. That's why we call it cheating.

✳ Current storage space that can't be fully used. This would include closets where there's more space than necessary above the top shelf.

You don't need to convert every spot on your list into storage immediately. Identify the locations on your list that fall within the most clutter-prone areas of your home, and start your conversions there. Home-improvement stores, organizer stores, hardware stores, office-supply stores, and discount stores offer multiple ways to create functional, convenient storage out of any of the odd spaces in your home. Keep the list for future reference.

"Utilize every bit of space," says New York City architect Evan Galen. In a home office, for instance, "A space between a column and a wall might be only 9 inches wide, but that could hold a year's worth of paper on adjustable shelves."

Now you are armed with the corner-cutting secrets for keeping an orderly and clutter-free home. Combine an organizer's outlook with some inexpensive storage equipment and a penchant for cheating, and your home will be ready for a photo shoot in no time. Maybe not for *House Beautiful*® but surely for *House Pretty Darned Good.*

SPOUSE, KIDS, FRIENDS, AND HIRED PROFESSIONALS

One of the most delicious ways to avoid household cleaning is to get somebody else to do it. The work gets done, and you don't have to lift a finger.

Now, I know I'm sauntering into tricky territory that's rife with gender-powered land mines. That's because, historically, women have done far more of the housecleaning than men. We all know why—back in the Ozzie-and-Harriet days women stayed home and vacuumed the living room twice a day in their pearls and high heels. Several decades later, two-career couples are the norm, but women are still typecast as the primary housekeepers.

The situation is improving, though. University of Maryland research shows that women's hours spent at housework were cut in half between 1965 and 1995, while men's housework hours doubled. Research released in 2005, however, indicates that women on average are still doing 61 percent of the household cleaning. And they're really, really steamed about that.

So in this chapter we'll examine how to get your significant other to do more cleaning—particularly if he's doing an *insignificant* amount of it. And I'm here to tell you that you can achieve this and still have your relationship intact at the end of the day. (In the unlikely event that you happen to be male and carry an unfair cleaning workload, this advice will work for you, too. Just switch the pronouns around.) We'll also examine how to get the kids to provide more cleaning help. And remember, hiring professionals to clean your home is actually a reasonable approach for many beleaguered couples.

Escaping the Gender Trap

If you want help with cleaning the house, you're going to have to ask for it. There is a whole complex of reasons why you got stuck with an unfair share of the cleaning. To turn the situation around will require a little gumption and some communication skills—applied in the right place, at the right time.

First, consider this news flash: Men and women are different! Apparently, you and your spouse are on different planets, looking at the cleaning issue through two vastly different lenses. Do *not* expect your spouse to share your priorities for cleaning, to use the same methods you would use, or to clean to your specifications.

"Men don't see dirt the same way that women do," says Sandra Beckwith, the author of *Why Can't a Man Be More Like a Woman?* If children spill a little fruit juice in front of the refrigerator, a woman will leap for the paper towels. The spill will make enough of an impression on the husband so that he avoids stepping in it, but it won't register as something that needs to be cleaned up. "I think it's truly a genetic thing—their brains aren't wired to see it," Beckwith says.

Upbringing also is a factor. Many girls are brought up with housekeeping woven into their play, whereas boys emulate Dad sitting on the couch watching sports. Thus gender stereotypes get perpetuated.

Here are other ways that men and women differ when it comes to cleaning:

PRIORITIES. A clean and tidy home is not a priority for men. Women know that cleanliness in the home is better for health and that furnishings last longer when they're clean. Women in general are more attuned to health issues and are usually the health-care brokers in the home.

RESEARCH. Women will read instructions on the label of a disinfecting cleaner. Men will just use the product—or ask a woman how to.

TECHNIQUE. Men approach a cleaning task like a military assault. Beckwith pictures a guy entering the bathroom wearing goggles and a bulletproof vest, a sponge in one hand and a spray bottle in the other. He sprays everything in sight, wipes quickly, and backs out fast. Women will take several cleaning products and tools into the bathroom for different purposes, and will do the cleaning slowly and methodically.

ATTENTION. Men come equipped with special filters that prevent certain information from reaching the brain. Hard as it is to believe, your spouse may truly not know where the mop is.

ASKING YOUR SPOUSE FOR HELP

Once you appreciate the gender differences with respect to cleaning, you're ready to ask for more help. "You're going to be resentful, tired, and cranky if you're doing it all yourself," says Susan Newman, Ph.D., a social psychologist at Rutgers University

STUPID MEN TRICKS

Author and speaker Sandra Beckwith likes to regale audiences with her collection of "Stupid Men Tricks"— goofy things that guys do and women would never consider. Where does she get her material? Unfortunately, everywhere she turns.

On a radio call-in show, for instance, the male types were just lining up to outdo each other. One fellow recalled that when he was single he used to stuff his dirty socks into a drinking glass, run the glass through the dishwasher, and then put on the socks and drink out of the glass. Another caller said he was above that—this superior being liked to dry his T-shirts in the microwave, flipping them over every 10 seconds to dry them evenly. As they say, guys, don't try this at home.

"Now you see why I stress the importance of training," Beckwith says. "If that's how they do laundry, they need help."

and author of *The Book of No: 250 Ways to Say It—and Mean It.* "If he doesn't see that, you're going to have to tell him—that you're not his maid."

If you're newly married, it's important that you and your mate have a full and frank discussion about dividing up the household chores evenly, says Jen Singer, a parenting writer and a stay-at-home mom. Think of it this way—you're establishing patterns that will last for decades. It's a lot easier to agree on an equitable division of labor in the glow of an early relationship than it will be to change entrenched habits years from now. Furthermore, if you take on too much of the cleaning, you're going to be overwhelmed when you have children. So make a detailed list of all of the cleaning duties that need to be done in the home and divide them up—each of you getting some chores you enjoy, as well as some that are nasty. Chart out who's going to do each duty and how often it will be done.

If you've been married for years, and it's time to redistribute the workload, plot out in advance the discussion points you want to make, approach your spouse in an rational state of mind, and spell out the housework situation—what needs doing and who's currently doing what. Tell your spouse that the workload looks uneven, and tell him how that makes you feel, says Beckwith. (*Pop quiz:* Which phrase is less emotionally charged: "burdened" or "pissed off"?) Remark that it looks as if he had more leisure time than you do—you want extra time to spend with your husband and less time vacuuming. Ask which duties he would like to take on—and let him decide. Again, it will help if the two of you work together to make a list of the cleaning chores, assign your name or his name to each task, and note how frequently each will be done.

Following are other ways to make sure that cleaning chores shift from your to-do list to your spouse's.

MAKE YOUR WORK VISIBLE Does your spouse have a Magic Underwear Drawer? He puts used undies into a hamper and clean ones materialize in the dresser! No, no, no. You need to find subtle ways to remind your spouse of all of the work you do, says Singer. So if you're going to launder his clothes, deliver

---

FIVE VERY MANLY
THINGS ABOUT CLEANING

If you're the kind of guy who fears that housecleaning is a threat to your manliness, here are five points to keep in mind:

1. Being in charge of a cleaning job is a valid excuse to buy tools.

2. When you clean, you get to wear your rattiest jeans, T-shirts, and sneakers.

3. A guy who can clean is able eat all the junk food on the couch that he wants—and hide the evidence.

4. Any guy who can leap into action at a party and remove a fresh wine stain from the carpet will impress the heck out of everybody.

5. You get to hunt down and kill fierce wildlife. Okay, we're actually talking about germs, but they're still dangerous little beasts.

his laundry in a basket to the bedroom—but let him put everything away. Also, when the two of you are relaxing in the den in the evening, having the "How did your day go?" discussion, don't hesitate to list all of the cleaning chores you accomplished. You did the work, so take the credit.

PICK THE RIGHT TIME Discuss your need for more help at a time when your spouse won't be distracted or resentful—not while he's watching his favorite sports team on television and not the moment he gets home from work and needs to unwind. Otherwise, an angry undercurrent will scuttle your discussion.

PROVIDE TRAINING Women often know exactly how to perform cleaning functions, but men often don't, Beckwith says. Tell your spouse the key things he needs to know about loading the dishwasher, for instance. ("There are men who load the dishwasher with the glasses face up," she says.) Make sure he knows where the detergent is, how much to put into the dispenser, and how to operate the controls. Provide any training by *showing* how it's done—not telling.

LOWER YOUR STANDARDS This may sound condescending, but it's not. Some women's standards for cleaning are "ridiculously high," says Beckwith. If you criticize your spouse's cleaning efforts or redo his work, he'll quit helping. Be happy that some amount of cleaning was accomplished, even it it's not the way you would have done it.

STICK TO YOUR GUNS If your spouse is supposed to handle a particular cleaning task and he doesn't get around to it, don't do it for him, says Newman. That's a trap: The workload will drift back to the same old inequitable arrangement.

SCHEDULE THE WORK Your grandmother probably had a rigid schedule for housekeeping duties—there was a wash day and an ironing day each week, for instance. Modern homemakers tend to approach their tasks randomly as they find the time, says Singer—and that often means that work piles up undone. Small, self-imposed deadlines will help you and your spouse keep up with the work. For instance, Singer makes sure she has all of the breakfast dishes put away in the dishwasher before the kids leave for school in the morning, and she changes the bed sheets every Tuesday.

PRAISE AND REWARD No matter how lacking your spouse's clean-ing effort might have been, find something nice to say about the job—and throw in a reward: "Wow, shiny bathroom faucets! Why don't we drop the housework for now and go to a movie?"

GET SELECTIVE WITH YOUR CLEANING If you're having trouble making your point about needing help, ensure that any duties that specifically affect your hus-band get done last or not at all—washing his clothes, sorting his socks, and picking up his shirts from the dry-cleaner, for instance. "Sorry about that, Herb—I had to vacuum *the entire house* today by myself."

TRY EXTORTION If your spouse is reluctant to do his share of the cleaning, says Beckwith, hire a housekeeper to alleviate the burden—once every 2 weeks might be all the relief you need. Also, take the family's dirty clothes to an outside laundry for clean-ing and folding. Hire a cook for a day to prepare a week's worth of meals (do an Internet search for "personal chef services.") If your spouse objects to these expenses, remind him that you've been asking for help. This will motivate your spouse to do more.

A DIRTY STORY

XXX

WORLDS APART

When you stay at home with the children, you and your spouse are often living in different worlds. Parenting writer and stay-at-home mom Jen Singer borrowed her husband's car once and accidentally dribbled some sesame seeds from a bagel onto the clean floor. (It's clean because the kids are rarely in his car.)

In good-natured retaliation, her hus-band sneaked into Jen's car and poured a half bottle of sesame seeds onto the floor. He sat back and waited for a reaction—and waited, and waited. You see, Jen's car is the prime vehicle for transporting the kids; it's a rolling museum of soccer balls and juice boxes. When hubby finally mentioned the seeds, Jen reports, "I said, 'Are they next to the lollipop sticks or the sand from the beach?' I didn't notice."

SANTA, RELATIVES, AND FRIENDS

During the gift-giving holidays in many industrialized countries, consumer spending goes into absurd hyperdrive. How many more scarves, gloves, and ties can our closets handle? How many more swirling, chopping, and grilling gizmos can we cram into our pantries? Do you really need a cell phone, iPod™, or digital camera that's only one generation improved over the one you already have? Here's a thought that will help return some sanity to gift giving: Why don't we redirect some of that spending in a way that will lighten our cleaning workload and thereby relieve some stress—particularly around the holidays?

Imagine this scenario: A couple decides that rather than dumping money into unneeded jewelry and neckwear for Christmas, they will spend a couple hundred dollars on a cleaning service that will scour the household from top to bottom. They have itdone in mid-December and can entertain guests hassle-free during the coming weeks.

Or try this variation: You and your spouse decide to have a cleaning service visit your home once a month during the coming year. Start up a cleaning kitty, tossing in some of that cash you would have spent on unnecessary merchandise. Invite your

in-laws to contribute as well (in lieu of the annual fruitcake gift).

Singer remembers fondly when she was a totally exhausted mom with a baby and a toddler in the house. Her mother took pity on her and hired a cleaning service to do a thorough, top-to-bottom cleaning of the house. That left only light maintenance cleaning for weeks to come.

The yellow pages and the Internet will put you in touch with professional house cleaners in your vicinity. However, the most reliable way to find a good house cleaner is word of mouth, says Judi Sturgeon, a professional house cleaner and home health aid based in Ambler, Pennsylvania. Ask your friends, neighbors, and co-workers for the names of people who do excellent work.

There's one big warning in this gift-giving business, notes Beckwith, and it returns to the issue of gender differences: Under no circumstances should a man give a woman a cleaning device or a kitchen appliance—unless she specifically asks for it. Men sometimes forget this crucial detail because they like practical gifts.

LITTLE PEOPLE, BIG HELPERS

Do your kids drift dreamily through family life like wealthy guests at a sun-drenched beach resort? Do they toss dirty shirts into the corner of the room only to have them reappear fresh and clean on a closet hanger the next day? Do they have a clue how to open the dishwasher? Do they turn green and yell "Mom!" at the first glimpse of cat vomit?

As long as you're redistributing the cleaning duties in the home, include the kids in the process. From a mercenary point of view, children are a good source of low- or no-cost labor. But they need to learn how to clean for their own good as well, says Newman. You're training them to be competent adults.

FINDING THE RIGHT WORDS

Explain to your kids that cleaning the house is one of the things they have to do as a member of the family. Most children have no idea what life is like within other families, so you actually have a free hand in deciding how yours will operate. "If you set patterns and standards, this is what they grow up with and this is the way they think life is. As a parent, this is your prerogative," says Newman.

Explain to your children the problems involved in keeping the house clean, and involve them in finding solutions. They'll take more ownership of those solutions and participate more willingly. As with your spouse, make sure your children have the tools and the training they need to do each cleaning job well.

You will probably get occasional whining, back talk, and dragging of feet. But be firm on these points, says Newman: Tell them no is not an answer, and that later is not an option. Say, "We're your parents. We're not your friends. You can tell a friend

MAID TO ORDER

Choosing a housecleaning service depends on your personal preferences and circumstances. Your biggest decision involves whether to hire an independent individual to clean your house or a full-blown housecleaning business, says parenting writer Jen Singer. Keep these factors in mind:

* A service that has several employees will always be able to show up on time. If they send in a team, the work will get done faster. The service may have specialists who will do a particularly good job cleaning such features as carpeting or upholstery. You won't know the workers, however, and the job will probably cost more.

* If you use a single, independent house cleaner, you'll know the worker and be more comfortable with that individual in your house. The job probably will cost less, and the worker will be more willing to handle odd tasks for you—such as taking phone messages or running errands. However, with one worker, the cleaning will take longer, and if that housekeeper gets sick or delayed the work won't get done.

you're not going to play, but you can't tell your parents you're not going to pitch in."

Most children are very adaptable, and they have a strong desire to please their parents, Newman says. "If a parent just says, 'I need help,' that often will get a child to pitch in." When you praise their efforts, they'll be more willing to participate, too.

Put the kids' duties on a chart in a prominent place—on the wall in the kitchen, for instance. Include in the chart the chore to be done, the child who will do it, and the day it's to be done. (When possible, use classy names for the duties—"Chef's helper," for instance.) To prevent squabbling, rotate these responsibilities weekly or monthly.

A WRINKLE SOLUTION FOR YOUR LITTLE SQUIRTS

Children are not renowned wardrobe planners. How many times has your daughter pleaded with you, just before bedtime, to iron a wrinkly blouse—because she's just gotta, gotta, gotta wear it to school the next day?

Author and speaker Sandra Beckwith knows the scenario well. Forget that hassle of setting up the ironing board and heating up the iron, she says. Put the blouse on a hanger, spritz it with wrinkle-release spray, and smooth the fabric with your hands. By morning the blouse will be dry and wrinkle free.

Wrinkle-release spray also is a blessing for travelers who want to make their suitcase-squashed clothing presentable.

"It has totally transformed how we do laundry," Beckwith says.

When the kids do their jobs, keep your feedback positive. Don't fret if a T-shirt isn't folded just so or they missed a dust bunny in the corner of the living room. "Don't get too hung up on quality," says Beckwith. "You have to lower your standards once in a while or your head will explode."

Should you reward your children for cleaning? Theories about this vary widely from family to family. One reasonable approach: Establish a specific set of basic duties for your children that they will not be rewarded for—that work is just part of being a family member. If the kids get their basic chores done and do extra cleaning as well, that deserves a reward—money, extra privileges, treats, or a movie.

AGE-APPROPRIATE CHORES

Want your children to be happy little helpers around the house? Make sure they have a reasonable chance of performing their cleaning chores well—with training and supervision, of course. Here's a look at duties that children can start tackling at various ages, according to experts:

1. **PRESCHOOLERS:** Take plastic plates to the sink, help set the table, put toys away, put coats away, dust (within reach).

2. **AGES 5–8:** Make bed, put book bag in order, put clothes in hamper, set table, rinse dishes, load dishwasher, wash pots, some bathroom cleaning, rake leaves, shovel snow, sweep.

3. **AGES 9–11:** Sort laundry, vacuum, dust, take out garbage, clean windows, scoop out cat litter boxes.

4. **AGES 12 AND UP:** Just about any cleaning duty, including running dishwasher, cleaning bathroom, laundering clothes.

APPEAL TO THEIR PLAYFUL SPIRITS

Kids are naturally fun-loving creatures. They'll help you clean the house more readily if there are playful aspects built into the work. Try some the following approaches.

PLAY BEAT THE CLOCK Set a timer for 10 minutes and tell your kids, "If we can get this room clean before the timer goes off, we'll go out for ice cream." You might not even have to use a reward system, says Sturgeon—often kids just like racing against the clock.

MAKE IT A TEAM SPORT Children will enthusiastically help with the cleaning if they're competing against others, says Beckwith. Have your spouse take one child to clean the upstairs bathroom while you have another child cleaning the downstairs bathroom. Provide each team with a checklist of tasks to accomplish and the tools to do the job—then shout, "Go!"

STRIKE UP THE BAND Lively music will inspire your kids to keep moving as they clean. Crank up the stereo or let them wear their iPods.

GET SILLY To make the chores more fun, break out the Halloween costumes and let each person dress up in an absurd outfit while you all clean. Try this while you rake leaves in the front yard—the neighbors will giggle about it for years.

TURN TOOLS INTO TOYS Let children have fun with their cleaning tools. Some kids like to play with the bubbles while they wash dishes in the sink, for instance, and others enjoy writing their names in the bathtub with foamy cleaner.

Now you are fully equipped to call in reinforcements. Sure, some of your family members may be touchy about taking on more cleaning; but you have feelings, too, and you deserve relief. An extra pair of hands around the house is too great an asset to ignore.

SANITATION *AND* SANITY:
KITCHENS AND BATHROOMS

Usually, the veteran, card-carrying cheater at house cleaning is happy to ignore that which cannot be seen by himself or guests. There is a significant caveat to this philosophy, however. Sanitation, health, and safety have to be based on science—not on corner cutting and looking the other way. We stay sane by concentrating on our top priorities, and this has to be one of them.

The cheating in this chapter, then, lies in maintaining laser-sharp focus on what's important and casting aside what's not. Fortunately, the secrets of sanitation around the house are simple and easy. By instituting a few basic practices, you can protect yourself from many of the germs that are lurking in your home. There are a lot of myths about home sanitation, too, so this chapter also provides plenty of ways to save yourself effort and angst.

You'll find much of this chapter devoted to sanitation where household germs do the most damage—in kitchens and bathrooms. You can't see these germs, of course, so we do the next best thing—attack the specific spots in your home where scientists tell us they are most likely to be. And, once your empire is secure from microbial invasion, you'll find shortcuts for keeping your kitchen and bath presentable and orderly.

GIVE GERMS A ONE-TWO PUNCH

Bacteria can live for hours on surfaces and viruses can survive for days. People who touch those surfaces can easily transfer those germs to their mouths and become sick; keep them clean and you seriously reduce the risk of food poisoning, flu, colds, and other maladies. Your number one defense in this battle is a commercial product called disinfecting cleaner.

Notice that the term *disinfecting cleaner* has two words in it. They're both important—a chemical tag team. First, check the label of your product and make sure that it uses the term *disinfect*. Use of this word has to meet Environmental Protection Agency (EPA) standards, and it means that the product kills bacteria and viruses. The term cleaner is crucial, too, because you want chemicals that are designed to loosen dirt from the surfaces that soil clings to. This way, the disinfectant can to do its job better. A disinfectant without cleaner is designed for use on surfaces that have already been cleaned. A cleaner without disinfectant is designed only to remove dirt, and the label of such a product will not promise to kill germs.

You can buy disinfecting cleaners wherever cleaning products are sold, including supermarkets, home stores, and discount stores. You could mix your own, but the commercial products are more convenient and provide

PUT THE SQUEEZE ON SPONGES

If he were to be reincarnated as a salmonella bacterium, microbiologist Charles Gerba would want to make his home on a kitchen sponge. It's dark inside, it's moist, it's got tiny traces of food embedded in it, and you smear it all around the room, providing plenty of places to multiply. Germ heaven! Well-intended housekeepers everywhere are wiping down myriad surfaces with a sponge, thinking they're cleaning—when in reality, they're providing a job relocation service for salmonella, *E. coli,* and other microbial creeps.

"Some of the cleanest kitchens we found were actually those of bachelors," Gerba says. Among the reasons: They used their sponges less and therefore spread fewer germs.

The good news is that de-bugging your kitchen sponge is easy. You just have to remember to do it. Any one of these methods will work:

❁ If you're regularly using your kitchen sponge to wipe up after using a disinfectant cleaner you're golden. Your sponge is no longer a bacteria colony.

❁ Equally labor free: Buy antimicrobial sponges, available in supermarkets and discount stores.

❁ Put your kitchen sponge in the dishwasher just before you wash a load. Germs can't take that kind of heat. Make sure you secure the sponge so it doesn't get snagged in the inner workings of the dishwasher.

❁ Dampen your sponge and microwave it on high for 30 seconds. Take care when you pull it out—the water inside will be scalding.

precisely the right balance of ingredients, says microbiologist Charles Gerba, Ph.D., of the University of Arizona in Tucson, a scientist who spends much of his professional life analyzing household germs. "The homeowner doesn't have to be a chemist any more," he says.

Park a bottle of disinfecting cleaner under the kitchen sink and under each bathroom sink. Squirt this stuff every day on the commonly touched hard surfaces, including counters, sink, faucets, faucet handles, toilet handle, toilet seat, refrigerator handle, and cutting boards. This will take only you 8 seconds per room. Read the fine print of your product so you're clear on how it works. Typically, once you have spritzed the liquid on, you have to let it sit for a specific period to get the germ-slaying done, usually 30 seconds to several minutes. Then you wipe the fluid up, rinse your sponge, and wipe again with the wet sponge.

YOUR HOME HIT LIST

Here's a rundown of commonly contaminated spots and simple methods for de-bugging them.

While the principles of sanitation apply to the bathroom as well, most of these observations involve the kitchen because that's where most of the harmful bacteria are found. At least a third of the disease-causing germs in your home hitchhike there on raw food. Also, people tend to do a much better job of cleaning in the bathroom. "The cleanest object in the house is the toilet seat, because people are so paranoid about it," Gerba says. "If you're going to lick anything in the house, lick the toilet seat."

Since you can't see germs, the best you can do is disinfect where they're most likely to hang out, thus reducing your chances of encountering them. If you disinfect the following hot spots, you'll be far safer from disease than most families. Be sure to check out "Put the Squeeze on Sponges" on the facing page before using that sponge!

A SECOND SKIN

Buy a box of thin, latex (or plastic) medical gloves at your drugstore and park it in a kitchen cabinet or the pantry. These inexpensive, throwaway gloves will get you through innumerable messy jobs, in or out of the kitchen, and save you a skin-scouring cleanup afterward. Just a few of the uses:

● Handling potentially germy foods such as raw chicken.

● Keeping the indelible scent of garlic or fish off of your hands.

● Handling dead presents dropped at the back door by the cat.

● Messy crafts.

● Painting.

● Polishing shoes.

● Changing the oil in your lawn mower.

● Cleaning the toilet.

● Cleaning up vomit.

THE KITCHEN SINK Think of your kitchen sink as a basket of bacteria, contaminated by raw chicken, meat drippings, and food scraps, all warm and moist. If you're peeling a carrot and it falls into the sink, assume it's contaminated and wash it off with hot water. Include the sink in your daily spray-and-wipe with disinfectant cleaner.

THE DISH TOWEL You mop up messes with it. You wipe your hands while you're preparing meals, smearing it with bacteria from raw food. Yes, your dish towel quickly gets as contaminated as the kitchen sponge. As part of your cleanup after a meal, switch to a fresh dish towel. Wash your dish towels in hot water with bleach. As with sponges, if you use your dish towel to mop up after use of disinfectant, the bacteria in it will curl up and die.

THE CUTTING BOARD Chicken, beef, pork, and even some fruits and vegetables wreak a peculiar kind of revenge when you cut them up—they leave bacteria behind on the cutting board. Think about this the next time you slice some chicken for stir-fry and then cut up a bell pepper. Do you really want to serve salmonella salad? At the very least, use one cutting board for your meat and another for your veggies during meal preparation. Then use disinfecting cleaner on both boards.

An easy alternative: I like to keep three hard plastic cutting boards available in the kitchen. After using one, I slide it directly into the dishwasher, which does a splendid job of disinfecting.

Wooden cutting boards won't stand up to this abuse, so I don't use them.

THE REFRIGERATOR DOOR HANDLE How many times do you pop the refrigerator open during meal preparation? Do you wash your hands first every time? No, you don't. A contaminated refrigerator door handle will quickly spread germs to every member of the family. So spray the door handle on all sides with disinfectant cleaner, wait the prescribed amount of time, wipe, and rinse.

TELEPHONES You might be surprised to hear that home telephones are abuzz with harmful bacteria. But think about it: You're putting raw steaks into a marinade when the phone rings. You pick up the receiver, you slam the phone down when you realize it's a recorded message, and then you hurry back to making dinner. You have just left a reservoir of germs on the telephone receiver. Disinfecting the phone is simple: Spray disinfectant onto a cleaning cloth and wipe the whole thing down—receiver, base, and buttons. (Don't spray directly onto any electronic equipment—the seeping fluid could damage it.) A disposable disinfecting wipe will do the job, too.

THE TV REMOTE Here's another popular microbial crossroads in the home—handled by many grubby fingers but rarely cleaned. As with the telephone, spray a cleaning cloth with disinfecting cleaner and give your remote a rubdown. Or use a disinfecting disposable wipe.

MORE SANITIZING STRATEGIES

Here are some more pointers, shortcuts, and surprising facts you'll want to know about sanitation in the home.

GO DISPOSABLE There's an easy alternative to kitchen sponges and dishtowels, which are famous for developing colonies of harmful bacteria. Instead, use nothing but disposable paper towels in the kitchen. "People say, 'Oh that's not environmentally friendly!' Well, if you get diarrhea and you use a lot of toilet paper, that's not environmentally friendly either," Gerba says.

WASH AFTER COOKING Here's a great item for the quiz shows: At what time during the day do you think people are likely to have the most fecal bacteria on their hands? Gerba conducted a study of germs on people's hands, and here's his final answer: After preparing a meal. People remember to wash their hands before fixing dinner, but it's not commonly done afterward, when their fingers are dripping with bacteria picked up from raw food. So scrub up with soap and warm water before you ring the dinner bell.

NO SINK? GO WATERLESS If you don't like scrubbing your hands at the sink so much or if a sink just isn't available, waterless hand sanitizers do a good job of killing the germs on your hands, Gerba says. They're available at supermarkets, drugstores, and discount stores. Keep a small container in your purse, briefcase, and desk.

On the other hand (sorry), don't be misled by dishwashing liquid that claims to be "antibacterial." Such labeling is somewhat deceptive, Gerba says. When you read the fine print, you'll learn that antibacterial dishwashing liquid is designed to kill germs on the hands—not on dishes. Many people use dishwashing liquid as hand soap when they're washing up at the sink, the manufacturers reason. To kill germs on your dishes, standard air-drying on a dish rack does a perfectly good job, Gerba says.

KITCHEN DISPOSABLES FOR MINIMAL MESS

Just about any time the food you're preparing meets a surface that you're going to have to clean later, there's a way to get a disposable object—usually paper, plastic, or foil—to take the "hit" instead. If this sounds wasteful, just remind yourself that letting food mess up your pans and counters has a cost all its own—you lose time doing the extra

THE GROUND RULES

You know the 5-Second Rule: When you drop a cookie on the floor, the thinking goes, it's okay to eat if you pick it up within 5 seconds. It's a time-honored, wishful-thinking rule of thumb for kids and grown-ups alike—usually cited as a way of excusing loutish behavior to by-standers. Well, you might get away with following the rule, but it has everything to do with luck and nothing to do with timing.

A food sciences intern at the University of Illinois at Urbana-Champaign decided to test the rule and came up with a surprising discovery. The floors she tested in high-traffic areas all over campus were relatively bacteria free, probably because the floors were dry and bacteria need moisture to live. You could eat an Oreo® off those floors.

Then the young scientist went into the lab and infected floor tiles with *E. coli* bacteria. When she dropped food onto those

tiles, the bacteria made the leap instantaneously.

So if you drop a cookie onto the kitchen floor, "It all depends where it lands. If it lands where the dog pooped, time is not a factor," says microbiologist Dr. Charles Gerba. "It is always a gamble with germs. Most of the time it is not a problem, but once in a while you lose. The way to play the game with germs is to always keep the odds in your favor."

In other words, the 5-Second Rule is a crapshoot.

cleaning; you need to use cleaning chemicals; you put wear on your pans, counters, and scrubbing tools; you use water to rinse it all away; and you use up energy heating that water.

Here are some delicious ways to cut corners while cooking, using inexpensive products that are readily available at your supermarket.

WAXING POETIC Just think of wax paper as a long stretch of disposable countertop. When you're cooking, tear off 8 inches and lay the sheet on the counter near the stove. After stirring the marinara sauce, lay your drippy spoon on the wax paper. The moisture won't bleed through to the counter. Use the same surface for grating cheese and peeling carrots.

Cover the kitchen table in wax paper when you and the kids are decorating cupcakes. When the icing starts flying, the table will stay clean. (The icing in your hair will still require a shower.) When you're microwaving an open bowl of food, lay a stretch of wax paper over the top to contain splatters and prevent a tough, cooked-on cleanup later on.

FOIL IT AGAIN Spare yourself the misery of trying to scrub baked-on food from your pans. Line them with foil every time you stick one in the oven. Pat Schweitzer, senior home economist for Reynolds® in Richmond, Virginia, says this is the quick-and-easy way to fit your pan with foil: Turn your pan upside down and tear off enough foil to cover it. Mold the foil over the pan. Pull the foil off the bottom, turn the pan right side up, plop the foil into the pan, and fold the edges over the rim.

A SAFETY NET FOR YOUR PIE Put a foil- or parchment-lined pan on a lower rack of your oven to catch drips any time you're baking a pie, says Jennifer Armentrout, test kitchen manager and recipe editor for *Fine Cooking*® magazine, based in Newtown, Connecticut. Throwing away a stretch of foil or baking parchment is a heck of a lot easier than cleaning the oven of sugary, baked-on drippings.

BAG THAT BIRD Oven cooking bags are tough sacks that contain the meat you're cooking and keep the juices where you want them—in the food, not decorating your oven, pans, and other cooking gear. The nylon kind works in the microwave or oven. The foil version works in the oven or on the grill. The large ones will handle an entire turkey, a leg of lamb, or a beef roast, and smaller bags will fit a chicken or pot roast. A quick search on the Internet will turn up hundreds of recipes that call for cooking bags and will revolutionize the way you use your kitchen.

GO SOLO "Hot bags®" are a close cousin to the oven bag. These are foil envelopes in which you can cook individual meals— say, a boneless chicken breast with vegetables. Not only are the hot bags disposable but they also allow you to vary the contents of the meal according to each family member's taste.

SLOW COOKING, QUICK CLEANING Nylon liners for slow cookers are yet another cheat-at-cleaning variation of the oven bag. Slow cookers (a.k.a. Crock-Pots®) are already a great way to cut corners in the kitchen—in the morning, just dump the ingredients in, cover, turn it on, and dinner is done when you get home from work. However, nobody enjoys cleaning that cooked-on crust of food from the ceramic interior bowl of the cooker. Nylon liners put an end to that chore. Set the liner inside the ceramic interior of the cooker and then load in ingredients as usual. When the cooking is done, serve the food, toss out the liner, and your slow cooker is clean and ready for storage.

SHAKE THE DRY STUFF The next time you need to mix several dry ingredients—for baking, for instance, or spices for stir-fry—pour them into a plastic bag instead of dirtying a bowl. To blend the ingredients, all you have to do is hold the bag closed and shake. Toss the bag out when you're done. If this is a recipe you make often, mix twice the ingredients you need. After blending, pour out what you need, then zip the bag closed, label it and stick it in a cabinet—all ready for the next time.

MARINATE IN A BAG Do you marinate meat in a large baking dish? You're setting yourself up for an unnecessary cleaning job. Next time, mix your marinade ingredients in a measuring cup, pour the mixture into a large zip-closing plastic bag, add the meat, and place it in the refrigerator. Set the measuring cup in the dishwasher and there's no more cleanup.

STEP UP TO THE PLATE

A funny thing happens after you've had your second child. Corner-cutting takes priority. Erik Sjogren calls them MacGyver^SM Moms—after the ingenious, ready-for-anything adventurer of television fame. These are the harried souls who see the wisdom of using disposable plates, cups, and flatware on a regular basis, says Sjogren, senior brand manager for Dixie® Tabletop, based in Atlanta.

Consumers traditionally look at disposable plates as an item for special occasions—picnics, barbecues, and quick snacks. Disposable dishware can work so much harder for you than that, however. To fully embrace disposable dinnerware, you probably need to get over two psychological barriers:

1. The notion that you're a Bad Parent if you don't serve your kids on your finest china. To heck with that. It's quality time—not quality dishware—that counts. If being able to toss out the evening's dinnerware buys you an extra 20 minutes to read to your kids, that's worth it. And that's the exact figure—Sjogren says research shows that using disposable plates, cups, and flatware at a full meal for a family of four saves you an average of 20 minutes. No plate scraping, no washing. Just run your arm along the table and push it all into the trash.

2. The notion that you're ruining the planet by using disposables. Well, favoring your ceramic dishware over disposables might not be as environmentally beneficial as you think. Washing a load of dishes in the dishwasher uses up several gallons of water and the energy to heat that water, plus it requires the use of cleaning chemicals, which get flushed away with the water. If use of disposable plates and cups allowed you to run your dishwasher every other day instead of every day, you would save at least 1,600 gallons of hot water per year.

J. Winston Porter, Ph.D., president of the Waste Policy Center consulting organization in Leesburg, Virginia, and former assistant administrator of the EPA, has closely studied the issue, particularly for the food-service industry. "It's not a slam-dunk to say you should always reuse," he says. There are a lot of variables, so you won't find a definitive answer, but he says the environmental impact of the two approaches is fairly equal.

Besides, it's getting easier to find environmentally friendly disposable goods. The paper plates I picked up at the supermarket are labeled "biodegradable in home composting," for instance. Watch the labeling for "green" products and encourage such manufacturers by voting with your dollars. While you're at it, do your wallet a favor and buy your disposable dishes in bulk at a wholesale club.

THE CORNER-CUTTING COOK

Abe Lincoln had it right: "Give me six hours to chop down a tree and I will spend the first four sharpening the axe." Use your brain, and you need less brawn. In terms of cleaning, this is particularly important in the kitchen—that daily maelstrom of veggie chopping, sauce slopping, and egg dropping. Aside from use of the disposables mentioned previously, here are more corner-cutting kitchen techniques.

WHILE YOU'RE COOKING

You remember the TWO philosophy from Chapter 1, right? It stands for Thinking Wins Out. During every second that you work in the kitchen, there is some way to make the cleaning chores go more quickly and easily. Playing a good-natured mind game with yourself will keep you on your toes. For every cheating shortcut you use while preparing a meal, award yourself TWO points on your mental scoreboard. After you use a cheat three times, it will become ingrained habit. You'll find your own shortcuts, of course, but here are some to get you started:

SAVE TRIPS Pile up three or more things—say, the wrapper from a block of cheese, trimmings from a bell pepper, and a garlic husk—to cart over to the trash can all at once rather than taking individual trips. A dozen steps saved. TWO points.

CLEAN AS YOU GO In that 30-second break you have while the onions are sauteing, clean off the cutting board, rinse, and set it on the drying rack. That's 30 seconds off your after-meal cleanup duty. TWO points.

MAKE YOUR PANS DO DOUBLE-DUTY Serve your enchiladas directly from the baking dish, then slide the leftovers, dish and all, into the refrigerator. That's a serving dish and a storage container you don't have to wash. TWO points.

CONTAINER CONSCIOUSNESS When you're hand washing a few items in the sink, put any larger bowls or pans in the sink first and sponge them out last. The smaller items you wash—say, a can opener and a knife—will dribble their soapy water into the containers, giving them an advance soak and re-using the detergent. TWO points.

BEFORE AND AFTER YOU COOK

Minimizing mess is not only a concern when you're in the heat of cooking. Here are some more brilliant kitchen ideas from the Ounce of Prevention Department, for the times between cooking sessions.

SHOP FOR THE CHOPPED Whenever you can, buy produce that is already partially prepared for you. This not only saves you work time in the kitchen but leaves your utensils, counters, and other gear clean. If you buy preshredded cheese, for instance, the grater stays smudge free. Prechopped veggies and greens are all ready for the salad bowls—no knives or cutting boards necessary.

MAKE A DATE WITH YOUR FRIDGE Refrigerators get cluttered because they're crammed full of items that may or may not be good anymore—nobody knows for sure, so nothing gets thrown out. Here's the simple way to fix that problem: Park a permanent marker near the fridge. No prepared foods—condiments, sauces, spreads, and such—go into the refrigerator without a date marked on them. So if you run across a bottle of barbecue sauce that was dated 6 months ago, you can toss it out without another thought. Mark the date on leftovers you put into the refrigerator or freezer, too. If you're using a zip-sealing bag, write the date on the plastic. If you're using plastic containers, apply a 2-inch strip of freezer tape and mark the date on that.

Before you make a grocery run, open the refrigerator and quickly review the fresh stuff: Toss out any aging fruits or vegetables; leftovers more than a day old get the heave-ho, too.

SLEIGHT OF HAND

BEAUTIFY YOUR BURNERS

Once a year, go to the appliance section of your home-improvement store and buy a new set of drip pans for your stove burners. Install them on your stove and toss the old ones. Keeping them clean is a hopeless task, and you'll never again be tempted to try. An alternative: Use your grungy old drip pans for day-to-day cooking, and slide in a shiny new set for use only when guests are visiting.

SANITATION *AND* SANITY

PUT YOUR FRIDGE ON ROLLER SKATES

If you could get behind your refrigerator without hiring a moving crew, you might actually vacuum up the dust that accumulates back there. The solution is simple: Set your refrigerator or freezer on a set of appliance rollers. These elongated roller skates are placed under each side of the appliance. With an easy pull, you can wheel the refrigerator away from the wall for cleaning.

Be ruthless—do not get sentimental over a browning pear that's squishy soft. For a deluxe touch, spray a little disinfecting cleaner onto your kitchen sponge and give a quick wipe to the surfaces you've cleared off in your fridge. The shelves in there are rarely more open than just before your shopping run. This will keep the interior of your refrigerator presentable until you get inspired to clear the whole thing out for a thorough cleaning.

CATCH THOSE DRIPS The juices from raw meat sometimes contain harmful bacteria—not something you want to spread around your refrigerator. So anytime you store meat in the fridge, put it on the lowest shelf to reduce the chances of the meat dripping onto shelving, other food or containers, says Jennifer Armentrout. Also, put a pan or other rimmed tray under the meat to contain potential drips—there are fruit and veggie bins beneath that lowest shelf, after all. "You don't want your meat dripping onto your lettuce," she says.

READ AHEAD When you're ready to start cooking, read ahead in the recipe so you know which ingredients are going to be added in at the same time. Those ingredients—wet or dry—might as well be mixed in the same container at the outset, rather than dirtying a number of separate containers. "That saves you cleaning a lot of little prep dishes," says Armentrout.

GREASE THE SKIDS Give your baking dish or pan a quick spritz of cooking spray if you're going to cook something that's likely to leave a crusty residue. You'll save yourself a ton of soaking and scrubbing time. If you give the cheese grater a shot of cooking spray before you shred your cheese, the metal will come clean with the quick swipe of a sponge. Before you fill a plastic storage container with a staining sauce (marinara, for instance), give the interior a shoosh of spray. The coating will prevent staining and make cleanup a snap.

A TRICK FOR STICKY STUFF Measuring thick and sticky ingredients presents a double quandary: It's hard to get all that molasses, honey, or corn syrup to pour out of your measuring cup—making the amount of ingredient imprecise. Furthermore, it's a mess to clean. Cooking spray comes to the rescue again, says Armentrout: Squirt the inside of your measuring cup with cooking spray before you pour in the ingredient. When you pour it into your mixing bowl, the sticky stuff will slide right out, leaving behind an easy cleanup job.

CONTAIN THE SPRAY When you use cooking spray, it's easy to spritz a little extra oil onto the counter or stovetop, creating an extra cleaning chore. Armentrout's simple solution: Open the door of your dishwasher and place the object you're going to spray on the inside of the door. Any extra spray that you get on the door will just wash away the next time you run the appliance.

GIVE FLOUR THE COLD TREATMENT Anytime a measuring cup or utensil comes into contact with dry flour, rinse it off in cold water, says Armentrout. Hot water turns flour gummy—a messy cleaning task. If you use cold water, all you need to do is rinse the flour off and possibly wipe with a sponge.

PRESORT YOUR SILVERWARE As you toss silverware into the dishwasher, keep it organized just the way you do in the silverware drawer—knives in one basket compartment, forks in another, and spoons in yet another. Doing this will take you zero extra time and, after you run the dishwasher, you'll be able to grab up a handful of silverware and drop it into the proper place in the drawer without having to sort.

RUB OUT POLISHING DUTY The next time you put your silver away, wrap each silver piece tightly in plastic wrap. If air can't get to the silver, it won't tarnish. If you'd like to spend a modest amount of money for more convenience, pick up a storage bag made of flannel that's specially treated to prevent tarnish. These are available wherever silverware is sold.

SMART CHOICES FOR A CLEAN KITCHEN

Think of all the inanimate objects surrounding you in the kitchen as chef's assistants— not only the appliances but the furniture and the trash can, too. If chosen and used intelligently, they'll save you a ton of time and effort.

WIPE OUT UPHOLSTERY STAINS The next time you choose upholstery for your kitchen chairs, ask the fabric store to send the material out to be laminated. The extra couple hundred dollars will be well worth it, says Deborah Wiener, an interior designer based in Silver Spring, Maryland. Laminated fabric makes wiping up spills quick and easy. The fabric also will last much longer, saving you the hassle of reupholstering in the future. If the word *laminate* reminds you of the hard-and-shiny surface of your driver's license, relax. Laminated fabric has a natural-looking matte finish.

LID LESSONS LEARNED When purchasing a trash can, make sure the lid will stand open by itself. You want to be able to toss in a trimmed-off broccoli stem from 6 feet away, saving yourself steps (and scoring TWO points). You don't want to have to touch the trash can during food preparation (you remember, germs). Lids that open with a foot pedal are a help (count on the mechanism breaking after 9 months), but that still requires you walking up to the can—steps you'd rather not take, if possible. The type of cover that swings on a center hinge won't do—it requires that you stand right beside the can and push against the lid.

POSITION BINS STRATEGICALLY Make sure your recycling bins are as close as possible to where the recycling materials are generated, says Cynthia Braun, a professional organizer in Lake Grove, New York. This means placing a bin for cans and glass in or near the kitchen. This ensures that refuse does not accumulate in inappropriate places.

THE MOUNT COUNTS If you ever have a choice about sink styles, go for the undermounted kind (also called an apron or farmhouse sink) in your kitchen rather than the drop-in kind, says Wiener. Drop-in sinks have a rim that sits on top of the surface of the kitchen counter. When you wipe the counter and push little bits of grime toward the sink, some of it gets caught against the edge of the sink and builds up over the months into a brown goo. With an undermounted sink, there is no obstruction and no dirty buildup.

MIND OVER SPLATTER On the stovetop, always use a frying pan or pot that's substantially larger than you need. This will help contain the splatter when the juices go flying. Just in case,

KITCHEN APPLIANCES: HANG 'EM

Before you buy any appliance that you plan to park full-time on your kitchen counter, look around for a model that can be mounted under the cabinet. Not only does this free up more counter space but your kitchen will look less cluttered and you won't have to move those appliances around when you wipe the counter down. Also, undercabinet appliances gather less dust, since there's no top surface for dust to settle on.

Microwave ovens, toaster ovens, can openers, and coffee makers are available in undercabinet models. If the chefs in your home need to be entertained while they work, drop by an electronics discount store for a clock radio, CD player, or television in an undercabinet design.

SANITATION *AND* SANITY

make sure there's an easy-wipe splatter guard on the wall above your stove. Whenever you can, cook in the microwave, where splatters are at least confined to a small interior that you can easily sponge off.

ARE YOU A FAN OF FRYING? When you fry food on the stovetop, make sure to turn on the overhead ventilator fan, if you have one. Otherwise, superfine droplets of oil will take to the air from your frying pan and waft about your kitchen, settling on walls, light fixtures, carpets, and more. This greasy film will build up over time, collecting dust and turning into a cleaning nightmare.

OPEN THE DOOR TO SHORTCUTS If your kitchen layout allows it, cook with the door of your dishwasher open and the dish racks pulled out. During the preparation of any meal, you'll find at least a half-dozen items—dishes, utensils, pots, and the like—that you use just once. Rather than setting those items down on the counter (which will then need cleaning) or in the sink (a temporary way station), put them where they'll eventually end up anyway—in the dishwasher.

BREAKFAST DISHES NEVER REST When you walk into the kitchen first thing in the morning, do you start pulling cereal bowls, plates, and glasses out of the cabinets for breakfast? Here's a better plan: If you turned on the dishwasher the night before, just pluck what you need straight out of the dishwasher. If you play your cards right, you'll rarely have to put the breakfast dishes away in the cabinets. They'll either be in use or in the dishwasher.

MAKE THOSE APPLIANCES CLEAN THEMSELVES

In the ideal cheat-at-cleaning world, every machine we owned would clean itself. Our only duty would be to kick back on the sofa until the little darlings were all sparkling clean. The good news is that we can get pretty darned close to that utopian state

GOING PLATELESS

Eating over the kitchen sink has a lousy reputation—supposedly the realm of slobs and lonely singles. However, sink cuisine shows a lot of promise for a cheat-at-cleaning enthusiast with tons of self-esteem and a burning desire to pare cleaning duties to the bone. Just in case you're unfamiliar with the particulars of dining at the sink, here are the steps for its most efficient execution:

1. Open the dishwasher and the kitchen trash can.

2. Wash your hands.

3. Get the containers of chicken wings and green beans out of the fridge, open them, and set them by the sink. (Reheating them in the microwave is optional.)

4. Get a paper napkin.

5. Lean over the sink, pluck the wings and beans out of the containers with your fingers.

6. Eat.

7. Don't set the chicken bones down anywhere—toss them straight into the trash.

8. Rinse your fingers under the faucet.

9. While the water's running, cup your hands to take a drink.

10. Wash down the drain any flecks of food that fell into the sink, then turn the water off.

11. Put the empty containers in the dishwasher and close it.

12. Wipe your face on the napkin, throw it out, and close the trash can. Belching like a warthog is optional.

CAN YOU DISH IT OUT?

Company's arriving in 3 minutes and you have a Pike's Peak of dirty dishes, pots, and utensils teetering beside the sink. What's worse, you don't have a dishwasher. What do you do?

Put all the dishes in the sink, add two squirts of dishwashing liquid, and fill the sink with hot water. Visually, this becomes "cleaning in progress" rather than "stack of goopy plates and flatware." Perfectly acceptable. To drive the point home, pull on a pair of rubber gloves when it's time to greet your surprise guests.

If you're desperate, hide the dirty dishes in the oven, unless, of course, the evening's meal is already occupying that spot.

with some appliances. Here's a rundown of common kitchen appliances and how they can actually help clean themselves.

BLENDER OR FOOD PROCESSOR Rinse it to remove most traces of food, then fill it halfway with water and add a squirt of dishwashing liquid. Close the blender or processor and turn it on for half a minute. Rinse again, then let the blades spin for a few seconds to throw off any remaining water.

COFFEE GRINDER Grounds left in your grinder can quickly go stale and taint the next pot of coffee you brew. Here's the easy way to clean your grinder after each use: Run ½ cup uncooked white rice through the grinder and throw it away. If you make a lot of coffee, just give your grinder the rice treatment once or twice a week. Other times, wipe it out with a damp paper towel.

COFFEE MAKER Put a new filter in the basket to catch any loosened mineral deposits. Fill the coffee maker's tank halfway with white vinegar and the rest of the way with water. Turn on the machine and let it run through its cycle. Turn the machine off and let the water and vinegar sit in the carafe for 5 minutes (to help clean the glass). Pour it out, wipe out the carafe, refill the tank with straight water, and run through the cycle again. Follow this procedure once a month if you have hard water.

DISHWASHER Cleaning the interior of a dishwasher usually isn't much of an issue—unless you happen to have those white deposits building up, indicating a hard water problem. This mineral buildup is not only unsightly but can interfere with the efficiency of the dishwasher. Use a product such as Glisten® or Jet-Dry® dishwasher cleaner often enough to keep the white streaks at bay. Put the cleaner in the washer according to the package directions and run the washer through a cleaning cycle. I use Glisten on my glassware to remove milky mineral deposits from those as well.

GARBAGE DISPOSAL Empty an ice tray into your sink and push all of the cubes into the garbage disposal. Then push a few lemon rinds down there, too (any citrus rinds will do). Turn on the cold water, turn on the disposal, and grind away until the ice and rinds are gone. The disposal will be clean and lemony (or orangey) fresh.

MICROWAVE OVEN Pour 2 cups of water into a microwave-safe bowl. Set it in the middle of the microwave and cook on high for 5 minutes. The steam generated will soften any cooked-on food splatters inside. Remove the bowl using oven mitts. Wipe down the interior with a damp sponge.

OVEN Self-cleaning ovens have been a common feature in kitchens for years. You have to follow the instructions for your specific model, but basically you run the oven through a superhot cycle, which incinerates anything on the oven's interior surfaces. When the oven cools, all that's left is a film of ash you can mop up with a sponge. Continuous-clean ovens are different. Their interior walls are treated with a chemical that will destroy small splatters at high temperatures (350°F and up). You still need to sponge them out once in a while and run the oven through a high-heat cycle occasionally, according to the maker's instructions.

GIVE YOUR
TOILET A DRINK

You've had a party, and guests have left several half-consumed cans of cola all around the house. Don't waste it! The acid in cola is a useful cleaner. Before you go to bed, pour a can's worth of leftover cola into the toilet and let it sit overnight. In the morning, brush and flush. Your toilet bowl will be bright and stain-free. Or pour two cans' worth of cola down a clogged drain and let it sit for at least an hour before flushing with water.

Don't use cleaning chemicals on continuous-clean or self-cleaning ovens. If your oven isn't trained to clean itself, it can still come pretty close: Pour ½ cup of ammonia into a glass bowl and leave it inside your closed oven overnight. Then pour out the ammonia and use a damp sponge to wipe up the grime loosened by the fumes.

LICKETY-SPLIT
KITCHEN CLEANING

No matter how many preventive measures you've taken to contain spills, splatters, and spouse, once in a long while you're going to put your hands on your hips and say, "This kitchen needs cleaning." I put the question to Janet Nelson, a Ross, Iowa-based spokesperson for The Maids Home Services: If you had a lavish 7 minutes to clean the kitchen, what precisely would you do? Here's a game plan based on her priorities. Gather your materials first, and keep moving.

1. Take that stack of papers off the counter and throw them into a folder to sort later while you're watching television. Toss other utensils, food items and such into holding baskets, cabinets, and drawers. Wipe down the counters. Nothing says "clean kitchen" like vacant counters.

2. Pick any kid toys or pet toys off the floor and stow them away. Use a whiskbroom and dustpan to sweep up any loose pet food.

3. Toss any dirty dishes into the dishwasher.

4. If your sink is now empty, spray it with disinfectant cleaner and wipe it down. Wipe the handles and faucet, then dry them with a dish towel to prevent spots.

If by some chance Venus, Mars, and Saturn should fall into alignment and you're in the mood for the deluxe *How to Cheat at Cleaning* 12-minute kitchen routine, do all of the above, plus:

1. Take the kitchen throw rugs outside and shake them furiously for 10 seconds.

2. Vacuum the kitchen floor and put the rugs back.

3. Spray disinfectant cleaner onto your sponge and wipe down the appliances.

4. Spray glass cleaner onto the window above the sink and wipe with a cleaning cloth or paper towel.

A THRONE ROOM FIT FOR A KING

If the Ladies Auxiliary were to devise The One True Test of Housekeeper Worthiness, they would probably base it on an inspection of your bathroom. Even knowing that in certain circles your reputation hangs in the balance, there's no way you're going to devote an hour a week to cleaning slavery in the throne room. Relax. Read on, and then invite the ladies over for tea and crumpets.

LICKETY-SPLIT BATHROOM CLEANING

Here's a 7-minute routine that will keep your bathroom looking harp. (Once again, a grateful toilet-brush salute goes out to Janet Nelson for her input.) As with the kitchen, gather your cleaning materials first and move as if you were meeting a deadline.

A CLEANER WITH TEETH

Denture tablets are a wonderful cleaning tool because they do their work with no scrubbing on your part and they can clean in places where you can't reach—or don't want to.

- Drop a tablet into the toilet at night, and in the morning you can just brush-and-flush your stain-free bowl.
- Fill the tank of your drip coffee maker with hot water. Drop in a denture tablet and let it dissolve. Turn the coffee maker on; once all of the water has dripped into the pot, empty it, then refill the coffee maker with fresh water and run it through its cycle again to rinse.
- To clean the crusty buildup in the bottom of a vase, bottle, or decanter, just fill the vessel with warm water and drop in a tablet.

Denture tablets can do their cleaning in as little as 15 minutes. In extreme cases, let them sit overnight.

1. Clear the counter of any extraneous objects. Put toothbrushes, hairbrushes, deodorant, medicines, toothpaste, and such into cabinets and drawers.

2. Squirt toilet bowl cleaner around the upper interior rim of the toilet. Spray the seat and exterior with disinfectant cleaner. Spray disinfectant cleaner on the sink, faucet and handles, counter, and tub.

3. With a toilet brush, scrub the interior bowl for 10 seconds. Flush.

4. Spray glass cleaner on the mirror and wipe with a cleaning cloth.

5. Using a damp sponge, wipe and then rinse (in order) the sink and its chrome, the counter, the tub, the toilet seat, and the exterior of the toilet.

6. With the same cloth you used on the mirror, wipe down the chrome once more for extra sparkle.

7. Tear off a 6-inch length of toilet paper to scoop up any loose hair and other debris from the floor and corners of the room.

As you've come to expect, for the truly finicky, I'm offering the deluxe *How to Cheat at Cleaning* 12-minute bathroom cleanup. Do all of the above, plus:

1. Put the tub mat, bath mat, and towels into the washing machine. Hang out fresh towels.

2. Vacuum the floor.

3. Empty the trash can.

4. Spray cleaner onto a cloth and wipe down the doorknob and the smudges on the door, the light switch, and the cabinets.

ZERO-EFFORT BATHROOM CLEANUPS

What, you're back for more? Okay, here are some more labor-saving tricks for the bathroom.

REFLECTED GLORY The mirror is a centerpiece for the bathroom. When it's sparkling clean, it's easier to forgive a hair or two

---

SWITCH YOUR FOCUS

Conventional wisdom would have you scrubbing the light switches and doorknobs in your home, on the theory that these are common way stations for germs in the home. Save yourself the bother, microbiologist Dr. Charles Gerba says. His tests show that light switches and doorknobs don't typically accumulate many germs.

He shatters a myth about public restrooms, too: Have you ever watched a finicky person, fearful of picking up germs, use a paper towel to open a restroom door? Relax. The door handle is actually the cleanest place in a public restroom. Another surprise: Among toilet stalls, the one nearest the door is typically the cleanest. People gravitate toward the center stalls, which are therefore the germiest.

left in the tub. Professional organizer Cynthia Braun likes to keep disposable glass wipes under the bathroom sink for a quick mirror-and-sink touch-up. C. Lee Cawley, a professional organizer in Arlington, Virginia, has a similar routine: Every night she uses a facial wipe on her face. Before tossing it, she gives the faucet and sink a speedy wipe-down as well.

TRY SHOWER POWER Here's another way to add instant sparkle to your bathroom: Pull down that old milky looking shower curtain liner and hang a fresh new one, says Braun. Yes, an old liner can be cleaned, but when they only cost a few dollars they're hardly worth the trouble. Buy a few at a time and count on replacing them every 6 months. If you're not in the habit of using shower curtain liners, now's the time to start—they'll keep the finer outer curtain clean and help it last longer.

SPRAY YOUR CARES AWAY Park a bottle of daily shower spray in your bathroom. When the walls are still wet after your shower, give them a spritzing. No need to rinse. The spray will prevent buildup of hard water deposits and mold. The shower walls will be one cleaning chore you can cross off your to-do list forever. Buy shower spray wherever cleaning products are sold.

SEE SPOTS RUN To keep hard water stains from building up on your shower doors, every few weeks dampen a cleaning rag with lemon oil or baby oil. Wipe down the interior of the doors. The shower water will sheet right off them, rather than clinging to the doors, drying, and leaving spots.

So there you have it: By adding disinfecting cleaner and a couple of disposable products to your shopping list—and then applying a little know-how—you get a germ-free, hassle-free kitchen and bathroom. Looks like the deal of the century to me!

6

WHERE YOU LIVE: KEEPING IT CLEAN IN THE LIVING ROOM, DINING ROOM, DEN, AND BEDROOM

In the ideal world, the living areas around your home would just clean themselves. Well, you might be surprised to find out just how close we're getting. If you make wise choices, a lot of the materials you use to furnish the living room, dining room, den, and bedroom will make housecleaning a snap. There are some time-honored traditions around the home you can dispense with, too, saving yourself a lot of housekeeping grief. And there are some amazing new cleaning gizmos that require no involvement from you whatsoever.

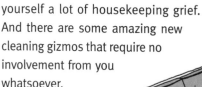

If you could remodel the main living areas of your home with only one goal in mind—to make cleaning chores as easy as possible—how would you do it? What flooring, furniture, paint, lighting, and window treatments would you use in the living room, dining room, and bedroom? I put the question to Deborah Wiener, a Silver Spring, Maryland, interior designer who is known for clever home solutions. Her answers deserve a prominent place in any homeowner's plans. Remember the Materials on a Program (MOP) philosophy: There's no need to accomplish all of these suggestions right away. Rather, factor them into your long-term cheat-at-cleaning blueprint.

FLOORING: THE HARD TRUTH

Let's start at the bottom—with floors. Stone flooring is the easiest to care for. Combine it with one of the new disposable mopping cloth systems, and you're on Easy Street. "You just take out your Swiffer® mop, and that floor's going to be spotless in five minutes," Wiener says. Use slate, terrazzo, or some other stone product throughout the house. If that's not practical, use slate for part of the home—say, the foyer, down the hall, and into the kitchen. Then use hardwood everywhere else. Hardwood flooring is similarly easy to clean, but it requires a little more protection (from grit and water). Stick to lighter woods, since dark wood shows dust and pet hair more readily.

Protect hardwood floors with strategically placed area rugs—for instance, by the kitchen sink to catch splashed dishwater. Highly colored and patterned area rugs will hide spills and wear-and-tear more effectively than solid colors.

BROWN DELIVERS For seating, chocolate brown leather furniture is "the ultimate in easy care," Wiener says. It won't show dirt or marks, and pet hair won't stick to it. When you're buying a leather sofa or chair, remember that not all leather is finished the same. Here's how to make sure the leather you buy is high quality: When the salesperson isn't looking, run your fingernail across the sample fabric. If it leaves a scratch, keep looking.

While we're on the subject of furniture: Buy chairs and sofas with exposed legs rather than the skirted style. The skirts attract stains and dirt from kids' shoes.

For shelving and other storage-type furniture, according to Wiener, "Anything closed is better than anything open." Look for an entertainment center with doors on the cabinets, for instance. Dust will not be able to settle on the objects inside, and closed cabinets are great for hiding clutter when guests come over.

WITH SHADES, YOU'RE ON A ROLL On the windows, forget curtains and blinds. For ease of cleaning, there's nothing like the old-fashioned roller-type shades. Modern roller shades are available in hundreds of attractive fabrics and styles. To clean, just pull the shade all the way down, wipe with a cleaning cloth, and roll it back into place. The newer cellular or honeycombed shades are very popular and energy efficient, Wiener says. However, they can trap dust—or even the little toys of mischievous children—inside the cells. To clear the shade out, you have to take it down, turn it on its side, and shake.

SLEIGHT OF HAND

INTERIOR WALLS: DUST IF YOU MUST

If I am ever caught washing the walls of my home with a sponge and pail of soapy water, would someone please just shoot me? Many of us have mothers or grandmothers who scrubbed their walls once a week, but life is too short. Sure, a little dust may cling to your walls. It's invisible, however, and will behave itself if you leave it alone.

If you insist on cleaning your walls, do this: Slap a fresh disposable electrostatic cloth onto your Swiffer mop handle (or whatever brand you're using), and give the walls a quick dusting. Start at the top edge of the wall and drag the mop head down until you hit the baseboard, some piece of furniture, or the family dog. Working your way around the room in this manner, you can cover a typical living room in 23 seconds.

While you're waving a dust-grabbing stick around the living room, you might as well snag any cobwebs against the ceiling. For a deluxe job, also drag the mop head along the top of each window frame and door frame.

THE 15-MINUTE TOUCH-UP

The phone rings, and it's your old college roommate wanting to drop by for a surprise visit—in 15 minutes! You gaze in horror around your unkempt living quarters. How will you ever cheat your way out of this one?

Focus mostly on the clutter, and then just one or two high-profile cleaning touchups, says Shannon Ackley, a professional organizer in Shelton, Connecticut.

- Throw the newspapers into the recycling or trash.
- Stuff books and magazines onto shelves and racks.
- Toss any toys into toy boxes or the kids' bedrooms—and pull those bedroom doors closed.
- Whip out a disposable wipe or dampen a paper towel with cleaner. Wipe down the bathroom sink and toilet.

Skip the vacuuming or dusting. A guest who's there for only an hour won't notice.

SCRUBBABLE IS LOVABLE

For wall paint, use only water-soluble, scrubbable paint. You'll pay a little extra for this in a premium flat paint, but it's unquestionably worth it. You'll be able to sponge up smudges and marks without fear of erasing the wall color at the same time. Flat paint is more delicate than the nail-polish-tough glossy finishes. Wash it using a sponge and a bowl of warm water with a squirt of dish-washing liquid. Use a light touch with the sponge, moving it in small circles against the surface. Use the same technique on high-gloss paint, too, before attempting a more stringent approach like glass cleaner.

Remember that darker wall colors will hide scuff marks and dents more readily than light colors. For trim paint, however, Wiener uses Benjamin Moore® Decorator White—not because she's a decorator, but because that color happens to be a perfect match for the correction fluid called Wite-Out®. She keeps a dozen bottles of it on hand so she can quickly touch up marred and scuffed trim.

SMUDGE-PROOF YOUR DOORS Doors attract lots of finger-smudges, Wiener notes, so paint your doors with a glossy finish, which will stand up better to repeated washings. Besides, wood looks better with glossy paint rather than flat. For hardware on your doors and drawers, choose a matte finish rather than a shiny finish. A matte finish won't show fingerprints. Only your CSI guy will know for sure.

DUST NEVER SLEEPS

Why do we call them "dust bunnies"? Do you think of the dust cavorting under the sofa as warm-and-fuzzy fluff? On the contrary, the dust in your house is a not so cuddly mixture of dirt and pollutants dragged in from the outside, fibers from fabrics, dander from your pets, your own sloughed-off skin cells, and even poop from dust mites. Inspired enough to fire up the vacuum cleaner? No matter how many corners you cut and tricks you pull, now and then you're going to have to actually clean something, and rounding up household dust is one of those core tasks you cannot completely avoid.

Fortunately, dusting is simple and easy. You can make a big impact on a room—give it that "somebody cares" look—with minimal effort. It gets complicated only when you throw obstacles in your own way—namely, clutter. So let's look at how to streamline this most basic of cleaning chores.

DUST BUSTING MADE EASY

Approach the room you're going to dust with all of your armaments assembled: the vacuum cleaner, electrostatic cleaning cloths (special dust-grabbing cloths available at supermarkets and discount stores), a Swiffer-type dry mop, and either a step stool or an extendable dusting wand that will reach high shelves.

Now, this will go more smoothly if you follow the "De-clutter, then clean rule." This means the couch cushions are picked up off the floor, the magazines are in their rack, the CDs and books are shelved, and the surfaces around the room are relatively free of odds and ends.

Once you're ready, an orderly set of procedures will allow you to accomplish a basic dusting of a typical living room in

FOCUS YOUR COLLECTION

There's a big difference between a collector and a clutterer, says professional organizer C. Lee Cawley of Arlington, Virginia. It's all in the presentation.

A clutterer has three Hummels displayed in the bedroom, two in the kitchen, and five in the living room. That's spread all about and unfocused—clutter. If you're going to have a collection, "honor" your prized pieces by doing it right. Put all of your collection in one display space (thus freeing numerous assorted surfaces around the house). A focused display place becomes a center of interest in the home, instantly changing that room from "Blah" to "Oh, wow!"

If you collect small, delicate objects, anchor each piece to its shelf with museum putty, available where art goods, containers, and collector materials are sold. With each piece securely stuck in place, you can clean them with a feather duster in just seconds without fear of tipping one over.

Leave 20 percent open space on your display shelf to accommodate new acquisitions, Cawley says.

6 minutes. For a *How to Cheat at Cleaning* deluxe job, well, that will cost you 9 minutes. (If you run over these times, either your room is too cluttered or you're trying too hard.) This dusting routine will work for just about any living area in the house:

1. Always dust from the top down, so that no dust you've knocked loose will settle onto an area you have already cleaned. Yes, you're using electrostatic cloths, which should grab and hold the dirt. However, if it's been a while since you dusted, there could be some escapees. Walk around the room in a circle, using your dry mop to snag any cobwebs from the upper corners of the room and using your dusting wand (or a step stool and a hand cloth) to wipe any high light fixtures, shelves, and ceiling fan blades.

2. Now, with a few clean electrostatic cloths, walk around the room in a circle again, this time dusting everything between your knees and your head—any shelves you didn't get before, the top of the television, window sills, and furniture. When one cleaning cloth is totally grimy, switch to another. Pay particular attention to any dust that's visible from a standing

or sitting elevation. (If you can see it, clean. Conversely, if it's not visible, it's optional.)

3. Run your mop or dusting wand along the baseboards.

4. Use your mop on any hard flooring. Vacuum any rugs.

You may now declare the room livable—unless, of course, you're going for your master's degree in housecleaning, in which case you would want to add the following enhancements to your routine:

1. Begin the entire dusting routine just outlined by moving all of the light furniture—chairs, end tables, standing lamps, magazine racks, and such—into the center of the room. When you get to the vacuuming stage near the end, vacuum around the perimeter of the room.

2. Put all of the furniture back into place.

3. Vacuum the center of the room.

4. Vacuum the sofa and chairs with the upholstery attachment. If there's time, use the narrow tool to vacuum around the cushions.

DUSTING EVERYDAY OBJECTS

Here's how to make cleaning go easier as you tackle common dust-collecting objects around the house:

PUT THE GRAIN UNDER GLASS *Pop quiz:* Which kind of surface is easier to care for—wood or glass? Glass, of course—just squirt on some glass cleaner, wipe with a cleaning cloth, and you're done. No special polishes are required, no anxiety about marks or water rings. That's why Cynthia Braun, a professional organizer in Lake Grove, New York, had every wood surface in her house covered in glass—desks, end tables, night stands, and dressers.

GREAT · GEAR

ERASING HOUSEHOLD BOO-BOOS

Oh, to be a school kid again—make a mistake, and all you have to do is whip an eraser out of your book bag. Wouldn't it be nice to have an eraser to fix all of life's boo-boos around the house, too—the marks on the floors, the cooked-on stove-top spills, the crayon scribbles on the wall, the smudged switch plates?

There is such a product, the Mr. Clean Magic Eraser®; and professional organizer Cynthia Braun of Lake Grove, New York, swears by it. "I have one of those under every one of my sinks," she says. She's particularly impressed that it easily cleans her white utensil holders when they get marred, grape juice stains on the counter, the grease-spattered teapot on the stove, and makeup smears on the telephone. It can make a wall look freshly painted and renew an old pair of sneakers, too.

Here's how it works: The eraser is the size and shape of a kitchen sponge, only it's white and stiffer. Just wet it under the faucet, squeeze out the excess water, and it's ready to clean. The pliable material of the eraser fits into the minuscule grooves of the surface you're cleaning and scoops out the dirt. Here's the big secret they don't tell you on the package, Braun says: It works even better if you use hot water.

When the eraser gets dirty, just rinse it under the faucet and squeeze again. After several uses, it gets crumbly. Toss it and get a new one. You can get them one or two at a time at the supermarket, but Braun likes to buy them in eight-packs at a discount store. It's not recommended for all surfaces, so read the directions and test an inconspicuous area before you do any large-scale cleaning with it.

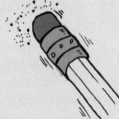

Go to the yellow pages and find a nearby glass company. It will send a worker out to measure your wood surfaces. The glass probably will be installed on clear disks that create a teensy gap between the glass and the wood so no moisture gets trapped in between. You'll be able to admire the beauty of the wood, but it will be perfectly protected and you'll never need to clean it again.

SHOWER YOUR SHADES Stop dusting all of those little crevices in your pleated lampshades. It's quicker and more thorough to give them a shower, says Braun. Once a year, remove the shades from all of your lamps. Place them two or three at a time in the bottom of your bathtub with the drain open, turn on the cold water, and hose them down with your hand-held showerhead. (If your tub isn't equipped with one, just turn on the shower and turn the shade under the spray. It might be less messy if you just strip and climb into the tub to do this—we'll never tell.) No scrubbing or detergent is necessary and you'll be happy to see all of the dust from your lampshades swirling down the drain. Let your shades air dry in the tub, then reattach them to their lamps. Even the standard pleated fabric shades come through this process just fine, Braun says, but don't try it on wood or silk shades.

SHOWER YOUR PLANTS, TOO Your houseplants will enjoy a shower now and then, too. They'll breathe easier once you've spritzed off that coating of dust that accumulates. Here's how: Set each plant's pot into a plastic grocery bag and tie the top of the bag loosely across the top of the pot, leaving a hole for the plant to emerge. Place the plants in the bottom of your tub with the drain open. Turn on a lukewarm shower for 1 minute. Let the plants drip dry in the tub, and then return them to their positions around the house.

PICTURE THIS: ONE FRAME ONLY Limit yourself to one framed photograph in your living room—or at least one photo frame per child. Why? One of the surest ways to cut down the dusting chore in your living spaces is to just put less stuff out. The fewer things you have on shelves growing that little coating of gray fur, the quicker your cleaning will be. Picture frames are a particular problem in many homes, says Braun. People feel like they have to display scores of framed photographs, and each frame has multiple edges and grooves where dust will gather—plus that dust-grabbing velvet backing.

Keep a photo album for each child in your family. When you get a new photo of one of your kids, slide it into the display frame. Put the old photo into the album. When the child reaches middle age, he'll love receiving the album full of his pictures. Because all of the photos were sorted to begin with, no one will have to tear up a family album to distribute them among the kids.

PUT YOUR MENAGERIE UNDER GLASS Keep your knickknacks inside a cabinet with a glass door. This way, your prized possessions are still on display, but you won't have to dust them nearly so often, says Shannon Ackley, a professional organizer in Shelton, Connecticut.

PLAY AIR PIANO Cleaning that piano in your living room is a tricky business, since liquid cleaners could damage the keys. The quick and easy approach, according to Braun: Blast any dust off the piano keys with a can of compressed air (available at photo shops and computer stores). When you're not playing the instrument or cleaning it, keep the keyboard cover closed to prevent dust from settling on it.

The compressed air trick also works nicely with computers and other electronics, cameras, and chandeliers.

SOCK IT TO 'EM Suppose you'd like to quickly dust a room but there aren't any cleaning cloths handy. No problem: Just pull a clean athletic sock over each hand and go around the room wiping surfaces. Start with the finer, less dusty items (knickknacks), then wipe the broader surfaces where you'll pick up more volume. When you're done, just peel the socks off and toss them into a laundry hamper (right side out, so the socks don't trap the dust inside).

POINTERS FOR PAINTERS

Painting—it's astounding how much of a mess you can make while beautifying your living room. Here are some corner-cutting cleaning tips that will make the job easier:

- Always paint with water-based acrylic paint, not oil-based paint. To mop up drips, all you need is a damp sponge.

- When you're done painting for the day, but you have to resume the next day, don't bother to wash out your brush or roller. Just wrap it securely in plastic wrap and put it in the refrigerator. This will keep it from drying out.

- If your plastic drop cloths have picked up paint splatters, as they usually do, don't be tempted to save them for the next painting project—throw them out. If you're painting with a used drop cloth, you won't be able to tell the dry paint from the wet. You'll drive yourself nuts trying not to step on the paint drops for fear of tracking them around the house.

- Always use plastic liners inside your metal paint trays. They're available wherever painting supplies are sold. When you're done painting, you can just throw the liner away and keep the clean paint tray. If you pour paint directly into the metal tray, you'll have a tough cleanup on your hands. You also run the risk that traces of the paint will taint the next color you pour into the tray.

- From head to toe, wear the rattiest clothing you have for painting —even for a 2-minute job. Paint has a way of leaping unseen onto your clothing. When you're done with the paint job, strip off all of these clothes at once and drop them directly into the washing machine. This reduces the chance of smudging paint onto furniture or other clothing.

- Unless you're obsessive about cleaning paintbrushes as soon as you're done with them, they're going to stiffen up after three or four uses. Life's too short to fret over paintbrushes. Expensive paintbrushes are an AILment (Anxiety-Inducing Luxury). Buy only cheap ones and throw the aging ones out.

There's more to cleaning your living areas than just dust. Here are some sneaky ways to outwit other kinds of grime.

SPURN THE BURN Quit using your fireplace. Boy, does it hurt to say that. I know as well as anybody the charm of a wood fire behind a screen in the living room. However, the science is irrefutable: Conventional home fireplaces are a terribly inefficient source of warmth. In some cases they actually *increase* your cost of home heating by sucking furnace-warmed air up the flue. At the same time, the typical home fireplace pumps fumes and particles into your home, polluting the air and making cleaning an even harder task. Also, dirt and bugs inevitably hitchhike into your house when you haul in wood.

The easiest solution is to have the flue of your fireplace sealed off and quit using it. Put a little candle arrangement in there, and light them when you get a hankering for flame. Alternatively, you could invest in one of the new, high-tech, airtight fireplaces that draw air from the outside for burning. Or you could explore converting to a gas fireplace—some designs are considered energy-efficient. If you're going to make such an investment, research thoroughly and don't believe everything you read in the sales literature. Also, modern airtight, advance-combustion wood-stoves can be a good alternative, providing low emissions and efficient heat transfer into the home.

GIVE DIRT THE SLIP When you outfit your couches and chairs with slipcovers, your furniture cleaning chores become a trifle. Slipcovers—essentially a second skin for your furniture—can be used in a number of strategic ways. Because they come in a wide range of colors and styles, you can easily redecorate your living room without buying new furniture. If the thought of the kids and Fido tramping on the new furniture ties your stomach into a knot, let slipcovers take the dam-age rather than the actual upholstery.

You can always remove a slipcover before guests come over, if you want them to see the splendor of the original upholstery. Or you can pull the slipcover off, give it a shake in the backyard, and put it back in place—no need to vacuum! If the upholstery on old furniture is worn and torn, the addition of slipcovers will add years to its life.

Most slipcovers can be easily removed and washed in your home washing machine. To prevent wrinkles, dry them until they're just slightly damp and then put them back on the furniture to finish drying. If needed, you can use a warm iron on the slipcover right there on the furniture.

Your slipcovers will have the best fit if you buy them from the manufacturer of your furniture. However, you also can buy slipcovers in retail stores and online.

USE GARBAGE CANS GALORE

When trash is extremely easy to throw into a proper trash can, it's less likely to wind up in alter-native places—on desks, counters, dressers, floors, and shelves, for instance. That's why Braun stations trash cans all over the house, particularly in the spots where trash is most often generated (desks, vanities where makeup is done, the scrap-booking and other craft areas, bathrooms, the deck, and the garage). If you station a trash can out on the deck or patio, make sure it has a cover to keep rain and inquisitive critters out.

LINER NOTES A trash can that's easy to empty will get emptied more often. You may already recycle your plastic grocery bags by using them as liners in your trash cans. Squeeze five of those bags into a tiny ball and put them into the bottom of your trash can. Then install another bag as the trash can's liner—over the other bags. The next time you need to empty the can, there will be another bag in the bottom of the can just waiting to become the new liner. No running to the pantry for a replacement liner. You can use this strategy in the kitchen, too, by putting extra kitchen bags in the bottom of the kitchen garbage can.

LET RUGS TAKE THE BEATING Your wall-to-wall carpet will develop a path of soiled and worn fibers in high-traffic areas. To preserve your rugs, or to cover stained or tattered spots, lay down runners in high traffic areas. Choose colors and patterns that will hide dirt well.

BEDROOM SECRETS

It's no wonder that people have strong feelings about how their beds are arranged. You spend a third of your life with sheets, pillows, and blankets all comfy around you in this one confined space. Make sure that your ingrained habits aren't working against you, however. You might be creating extra housework for yourself or, worse, you might be inviting some tiny, health-damaging creatures to snuggle up with you.

QUIT MAKING THE BED

Approximately 60 percent of people surveyed say they don't make the bed every day. Are they slobs? Not at all—they're visionaries.

Sure, some of my advisers insist that there's great emotional value in making your bed every day. A tidy bed is a comfort to the soul, the thinking goes, and makes a more inviting place to retire to at the end of the day. If that's all it takes to make your spirit soar, by all means give your covers a quick tug at each corner and be done with it.

Be aware, however, that scientists say *not* making your bed actually appears to be healthier. Why? Because the average bed can house as many as 1.5 million hideously ugly microscopic creatures called dust mites. These miniature monsters produce allergens that you breathe in while you sleep, and this is a major cause of asthma and other illnesses. A 2005 study unveiled at Kingston University in London showed that killing the dust mites in your bed is simple. The mites thrive on the moisture in your bed covers and mattress. When you make the bed, you're sealing the moisture in—tucking the little dust mites in just the way they like it. However, when you leave your bed unmade all day, the moisture escapes and the dust mites die. I'm sold!

FAST·FORMULAS

SHAVING CREAM, IN THE NICK OF TIME

If you need to fix a carpet stain and you're out of commercial spot cleaner, there's a good backup plan right in your bathroom cabinet. Get your can of shaving cream and three paper towels. Squirt onto your fingertips enough foam to cover the stain. Rub it into the stain with your fingers and let it sit 1 minute. Blot up as much of the foam as you can with one dry paper towel and toss it in the trash. Wet the second paper towel slightly with warm water and blot at the spot to remove any excess foam, then toss it. Leave the third paper towel dry. Fold it up until it's just large enough to cover the stain. Press it down onto the spot with your knuckles to soak up as much water as possible, and then throw it away. Let the carpet dry for a few hours, and then vacuum.

GET CLEVER WITH YOUR COVERS

Maybe leaving your bed unmade all day is too radical for you, even if it is scientifically sound. No problem—there are plenty of other bed management tricks that will protect your health and save you a lot of bother.

SKIP THE TOP SHEET At first this will sound nuts to many Americans: Quit using a top sheet. That's right. The conventional American way of making a bed requires a fitted sheet on the mattress, then a flat top sheet tucked in at the foot of the mattress, and

MAKING THE BED: LET IT SLIDE

If you insist on making your bed, at least amuse yourself by getting the job done before you're even on your feet in the morning. An item in *The Scotsman*, "Scotland's national newspaper," describes how to make the bed while you're still in it. The technique involves sliding out from under the covers at the foot of the bed, so it's assumed that you're not using a top sheet. Perform all of the motions described here slowly and carefully so that the duvet doesn't get dragged out of position. Here's how it's done:

- If there's anybody else in your bed, kick that person out—you have work to do. Lie on your back in the center of the bed, under the duvet.

- Spread your legs until you have a foot pointing toward each bottom corner of the bed. This flattens out the lower part of the duvet.

- Grab the top corners of the duvet in your left and right hands and give it a little pull.

- Slowly move one hand toward your chin, grab the center edge of the duvet, and pull it over your head—thus flattening the central part of the cover—and return your hand to its corner. The bed is now made—you just have to get out of it.

- Using a very slow rolling motion with your posterior, inch your way toward the bottom of your bed, taking great care not to disrupt the duvet. It might help to leave your hands higher than your head, smoothing out the duvet if it needs adjusting.

- When your feet hit the floor, slowly crab-walk forward. When your arms come, free, support yourself on all fours until you're clear of the bed.

It takes a little practice before you can pull this off without a hitch, but it will give the household rebel in you a definite feeling of accomplishment first thing in the morning. I stripped down to my skivvies to give it a try. We'll not repeat what my wife said when she walked in.

then a bedspread or comforter layered on top. Well, forget that top sheet—instead, just use a duvet. A duvet, for the uninitiated, is a cover for a comforter. They come in a variety of fabrics, colors, and patterns, giving you a lot of flexibil-ity with decorating. They also simplify cleaning: Your comforter never gets dirty—the duvet does. Removing the duvet and washing it is a thousand times easier than washing a comforter itself.

Having the duvet directly against your skin is every bit as comfortable as sleeping with a top sheet. If you dispense with the top sheet, you have one less thing to wash, and suddenly making your bed is markedly easier—just give the duvet a quick yank at each corner of the bed and you're done in seconds. Top sheets, on the other hand, often bunch up underneath the top cover, making the bed look like a topographical map of the Appalachian Mountains. Europeans will find nothing new in this advice, since they typically forego top sheets anyway.

DESIGN DIRT AWAY

TAKE COMFORT IN A DUVET

A duvet comforts your comforter—gives it protection, anyway. It also makes managing your bed a snap—it's easy to straighten and easy to clean. Here are a few things to consider about buying a duvet:

- A cotton-polyester blend is easiest to care for. A few times a year, remove it from your comforter and toss it in the washing machine, just like a sheet.
- If you're using a duvet, quit using a top sheet. Simpler is better.
- Make sure your duvet is a good fit for your comforter. Your best bet is to buy one from the same folks who made the comforter itself. If you're buying from another manufacturer, remember that standardized sizes (twin, queen, and such) are not reliable—take a tape measure to your comforter and buy your duvet according to actual measurements.

FIGHT THE MITE If you think dust mites might be a source of your allergy problems, you'll want to take extra measures to keep them away from you while you're sleeping. Here are two good moves, according to Jay M. Portnoy, M.D., the chief of allergy, asthma, and immunology at Children's Mercy Hospital in Kansas City, Missouri:

* Buy dust mite covers for your pillows and mattress. These covers place a barrier between you and the allergens.

* Wash your sheets frequently in water that's at least 130°F.

PILLOW TALK Pillows take on a musty odor after a while, and the surest solution is this: Buy new ones every 6 months to 8 months. If you'd just like to freshen up a stinky pillow, put it in the drier with a drier sheet. If you're willing to put more work into your pillows, most of them are machine-washable—check the tag. Even down pillows often can be washed in a gentle cleaner such as Woolite®. (If you bought dry-clean-only pillows, what were you thinking?) Just make sure that any pillow you wash gets really, really dry before you put it back into action. It can take hours of machine drying (gentle or medium setting) to get all of the moisture out of a feather pillow. To punch up the loft of down pillows, it helps to put a couple of tennis balls into the drier with them.

GO PLAIN AND FANCY If you have a hankering for elegant, designer-type bedding, limit these touches to the bed skirt, toss pillows, and duvet. For practical living, the work-a-day bedding underneath (the sheets and pillow cases) ought to be plain ol' white. Why? So you can easily bleach them if they get dingy or stained, says interior designer Deborah Wiener. You can buy high-quality white sheets at discount stores for a reasonable price.

COLLAPSE YOUR COMFORTER Storing a comforter requires a significant amount of closet space. To save room, fold your comforter and slide it into a large trash bag. Then put the hose of your vacuum cleaner into the bag, hold the plastic securely around the hose, and turn

the vacuum cleaner on. The comforter will be compressed to a fraction of its usual size. Seal the bag closed with a twisty-tie. Use the same technique for storing pillows. This extra closet space will translate into less clutter in your bedroom.

BEYOND THE BEDCOVERS

The bed is just 40-some square feet of the bedroom. Here's how to keep the rest of your inner sanctum neat and clean with minimal effort.

TELL THE TREADMILL TO TAKE A WALK If you're crowding an office, exercise equipment, and a television into your bedroom, chances are nothing is getting accomplished there. The desk is dysfunctional, the treadmill is covered in cobwebs, and you habitually nod off in the middle of that late-night TV show.

"Ideally, the bedroom should just be for sex and sleeping—and that's it," says C. Lee Cawley, an organizer in Arlington, Virginia. So give everything but your bed, clothes, and dresser the heave-ho.

BE A CLOSET GADGET JUNKIE Every chance you get, browse home-improvement stores, discount stores, and department stores for the myriad clever devices that save space in your closet and make items easy to find. For instance:

* A belt ring, which holds a score of belts while taking up a mere 2 inches of hanging rod space in your closet.

* A mesh bag. Fill it with small accessories such as earmuffs, bandannas, and headbands, and hang it on a hook in your closet.

* A compact step stool stashed in or near your closet (the folding kind can slide under your bed) will suddenly make the highest shelves of your closet easy to reach—and no longer a museum of forgotten items.

* A shoe bag mounted on the back of a closet or bedroom door will get that jumble of shoes off the floor. It's also handy for storing other small items, such as rolled up scarves, pantyhose, and gloves.

TWO RODS ARE BETTER THAN ONE

Double the hanging space in your bedroom closet by installing two hanging rods, one over the other. Hang one rod 40 inches off of the floor and the other at 80 inches.

GIVE YOUR HAMPER SOME AIR Don't store your dirty clothes hamper inside your closet. Not only will that rob you of a huge block of storage space but also those musty used clothes will share their odor with the fresh garments in your closet.

HOOK YOUR BATHROBE Mount a handsome hook on the wall near—but not inside—your closet, and park your bathrobe there. Bathrobes often get full of moisture during your shower routine, and an open-air hook will allow it to dry more thoroughly.

MORE CLOSET, LESS CLUTTER If you ever get the chance to remodel your child's bedroom, devote a large chunk of the room to a seriously expanded closet, Wiener says. Include in that closet generous hanging space, shelving, and other storage. This will limit the need for furniture out in the bedroom at large—thus cutting down on clutter, dust, and nicks and scuffs.

"To me, putting everything behind closed doors is preferable," she says.

LIGHT HOUSEWORK

Here's where I advise you to throw out all of the lamps in your house. Bear with me for a moment—I'm not crazy. Remember: Cleaning would be extremely easy, just 90 seconds of dusting, if it weren't for all of the obstacles that you throw in your own way. You have to walk around lamps, coddle them like babies, and—worst of all—

they are exquisitely designed to gather dust and grime, whether they're hanging lamps, standing lamps, or table lamps. Look into the upturned shade of your floor lamp. Check your wall-mounted sconces, those hanging fixtures, and the pleated shades of those table lamps. Cobwebs, dead bugs, and dust, dust, dust. Lampshades get old and yellowed, too, and need replacing periodically.

What's the solution? Install recessed lighting throughout your house, says Wiener. This is the type of lighting that looks like a coffee can embedded in the ceiling. Light shines down into the room, but there is no bulky object intruding on the *space* of the room—nothing to tip over, nothing to trip over, and nothing to clean.

Most folks would want to hire an electrician to convert a room to recessed lighting. If you have easy access to the floor above (maybe there's just attic up there) this is a surprisingly easy job, Wiener says. If there's a finished room above, it's still not a terribly involved project—you'll just have to patch some drywall in a few spots. "I do it all the time," Wiener says.

Sure, installing recessed lighting requires a small investment, but it's a move that will pay off grandly over the long haul. Use the MOP philosophy: You might not convert the entire house at once. Just factor recessed lighting into your planning for the home and get it done when it's most strategic to do so—when there are workers at the house anyway installing ceiling fans or remodeling the kitchen, for instance. You'll save on labor costs if the workers don't have to make a separate house call.

Use extra-long-life halogen bulbs in your recessed lighting, Wiener says—they'll last 2 years or 3 years without a change, saving you a lot of bother. Also, put all of your lights on dimmer switches. One set of lights could illuminate the room over all, and other lights could be focused—say, on work areas or over the bed for reading.

Light has an enormous influence on the perception of cleanliness in your home. Think of yourself as the lighting technician

AD-HOC CLEANING

A half hour television show will typically have 8 minutes of commercials—and sometimes as much as 12 minutes. Why not use those minutes to catch up on some cleaning chores rather than allowing yourself to be hypnotized by Madison Avenue? Making good use of this "found time" means you won't have to devote part of some future weekend to these tasks.

Think ahead and gather any cleaning implements you'll need before your favorite show begins. To get you started, here are some cleaning tasks you can accomplish during a 2-minute commercial break:

* Sort that messy pile of papers into stacks such as "To be filed," "Take action on this," and "Throw away."

* Take the "To be filed" papers to your filing cabinet and put each in its proper folder. Toss the "Throw away" pile into recycling.

* Take a clean, dry dusting cloth and wipe down the entire entertainment center, working from top to bottom.

* Spray a cleaning cloth with disinfectant and wipe down all of the telephone receivers in the house.

* Pull the couch 4 feet away from the living room wall, scoop up all of those dust bunnies with a dusting mop, and put the couch back.

for your own theatrical production. You can toy with numerous variations and combinations of lighting sources, but there are two basic modes that you need to put the most thought to.

BRIGHT-AND-FUNCTIONAL MODE

Sure, brighter light will illuminate the dust and dirt in your home. But that's okay, because you're going to use the bright-and-functional mode only for you and your family. If the lighting helps you see dust on a living room shelf, you'll put that little dusting job on a mental to-do list.

For your day-to-day living, be generous with light. Walk around your house and examine every work area. Make sure good, bright light is provided for the task at hand. This includes reading areas, the office, the kitchen, the laundry room, craft and sewing areas, and the workbench.

If work around the house is not getting done often enough or well enough, poor lighting could be a contributing factor. For instance, Cawley often finds that a client's kitchen table is cluttered with work papers—so there's no place to eat comfortably. The resident doesn't realize that she is instinctively using the kitchen table as a desk because the light is better there. The home office—where those papers belong—is typically in a dark basement, a closet or some other odd corner of the house. Fix the lighting at your desk, and suddenly the kitchen table will be free for dining.

Yes, use of generous lighting means more power consumption and therefore higher cost. To compensate, install compact fluorescent bulbs (they fit into conventional bulb sockets) wherever you can in your home. While these bulbs are initially more expensive to buy than conventional incandescent light bulbs, they're cheaper in the long run—they consume much less electricity and last for several years. Use of fluorescents or other long-life bulbs also means, obviously, that you don't have to replace blown-out bulbs as often.

Also, open the blinds and curtains to let plenty of natural light into the house. It's free, after all. Scientists say that exposure to natural light can help alleviate depression in some cases. I'm not saying that sunlight will give you enough of an emotional bounce to clean the entire house, but at the very least you'll feel better about not having done it.

DIM-AND-SELECTIVE MODE

The dim-and selective lighting mode is what you use when guests come over. Any clutter, dirt, or dust you didn't get around to will be undetectable in the dark. For entertaining, turn off the lights in all areas where you don't want guests to go—the basement, the bedrooms, and your office, for instance. In the areas where your guests will roam freely—say, the living room, dining room, and kitchen—use dim lights in general, with a few narrowly focused lights emphasizing some nice feature of your home. In the living room, this might mean turning on just one corner lamp, plus a small spotlight on a painting (you've dusted the frame, of course). In the kitchen, the light focused over the kitchen table is on (you have a nice appetizer spread there), but the brighter overhead light is off.

Such devices as dimmer switches and three-way bulbs will help a lot with dim-and-selective mode. As needed, you also can remove 100-watt bulbs from some of your fixtures and replace them with 60-watt bulbs just before guests arrive.

MORE BRIGHT IDEAS

Maybe you're not ready to convert every single room to recessed lighting. All right, I'll still help you find some low-maintenance lighting fixtures. Here are some ideas from Jeff Dross, product manager and trend analyst for Kichler Lighting in Cleveland, Ohio:

FOREGO THE GLASS You don't exactly have easy access to a light fixture that dangles 10 feet above your head in a two-story foyer. So it pays to remember this law of lighting: Any enclosed glass fixture will become a highly visible burial ground for bugs that fry themselves against the light bulb. You'll need a ladder or scaffolding to get up there and empty their dead little carcasses out periodically. Instead, pick the kind of fixture that has a metal frame but no glass enclosure. Then your only cleaning task is removing dust and cobwebs. You can buy dusters mounted on long, telescoping poles that will quickly clean such out-of-reach fixtures. Or just tape a duster to the end of a broomstick to get the job done.

WARM IT UP Select lampshades in warm colors, such as yellows and oranges, as the light they throw will reveal less dirt, Dross says. Cooler tones—grays and blues—produce a starker, less forgiving light.

DON'T DANGLE Don't buy light fixtures with dangling elements—crystal chandeliers, for instance. Dusting them is a hopeless chore.

A NEW TWIST ON CANDLE POWER Light bulbs that are shaped like candle flame, the kind typically used in chandeliers, gather dust easily—but they're a breeze to clean, Dross says. Just turn the chandelier off, spray some glass cleaner on a paper towel, and quickly twist the towel around the bulb. "You'd be surprised at how clean this makes the whole room look," he says.

LOOK FOR LACQUER Make sure any brass or copper in the light fixtures you buy is lacquered—meaning it has a clear protective finish that you can clean with the simple swipe of a cloth. Stay away from unfinished brass and copper, unless you're willing to just let them corrode. Such fixtures are intended for people with servants who spend their days polishing.

ROUGH SURFACE, ROUGH GOING Avoid light fixtures that have glass with textured exterior surfaces. This kind of trendy glass collects dirt and is a pain to clean.

CLEARING THE AIR

Have you ever met a woman who uses way too much perfume? You almost smother under the tidal wave of sweet fragrance. Her good intentions are actually working against her—and she's oblivious to the problem, because her nose has acclimated to a high level of that particular scent.

Your efforts to "freshen" the air in your home can backfire in the same way. If you have odor "issues" in your home, layering on yet another scent—even a pleasant one—can create more of a problem than you had in the first place. Ironically, you are the worst person on the planet to judge whether your home smells okay, according to Pamela Dalton, Ph.D., an odor scientist at the renowned Monell Chemical Senses Center in Philadelphia. While your nose might be accustomed to a high level of artificial fragrance in your house, guests could be bowled over by the odor.

So here we're going to talk about easy ways to manage odors in your home without smothering innocent visitors. First, it helps to know just a little bit more about your nose and what it knows.

Smell is an old, primal sense, Dalton says. We are not programmed to detect the scents that linger around us all of the time. Rather, we are programmed to pick up changes in the scents that are around us. That's because in prehistoric times the primary function of our sense of smell was to detect danger ("Uh-oh, predator nearby") or food ("Mmm, ripe berries"). Messages about odor are processed in the brain in the same area where we store emotional memories. You could say that odors are hard-wired to our emotions.

That is why real estate agents' odor tricks really work. You know: When prospective buyers are headed to your house, you bake a loaf of bread, put on a pot of aromatic coffee, boil a cinnamon stick in water on the stovetop, or place a drop of vanilla on a light bulb and turn it on. Any of these homey odors will immediately put buyers in a positive frame of mind, imagining your home as a place of family, food, and comfort.

However, don't go overboard with home scents. If you have a fragrance-producing gizmo jammed into an outlet in every room, it's probably time to unplug and rethink what you're doing. "I'm not a big advocate of using a lot of fragrance products," says Dalton. When you overuse a home fragrance, you might unwittingly create the impression that you have something to cover up. So easy does it.

If your own nose is not a reliable judge of the air in your home, how are you supposed to know whether you have odor problems? Ask a friend to drop by, sniff around, and give you an honest assessment, says Dalton. When you do, get right down to business—the human nose starts to get acclimated to its environment after only 15 minutes. Your friend can tell you whether there's a general mustiness about your home, an overwhelming floral scent, or if there are odor problems in specific places around the house—the refrigerator, the cat box, or a kid's closet, for instance. Make a "hit list" for remedial action.

Here's another easy way to get a read on your home's odor problems: When you return home after a week's vacation, what

A DIRTY STORY
XXX
EAU DE HOTEL

During a vacation, Cynthia Braun's husband stepped into their hotel room and wrinkled his nose. "This hotel room doesn't smell so good," he said.

Braun, a professional organizer, sniffed out the problem right away. During 16 years of marriage, her husband has gotten accustomed to the potpourri she spreads all over the house—plain ol' hotel smell wasn't good enough. So Braun whipped out her aerosol can of potpourri spray, spritzed the room, and the smile returned to her husband's face.

does the interior smell like? An overused gym locker? You may tell yourself that the house has been closed up and you just need to open some doors and windows to air it out. More likely, Dalton says, that's what your home really smells like to visitors.

SHEDDING LIGHT ON ODORS

Forget about air fresheners, forget about sprays, forget about potpourri. If you want the easiest, laziest, cheating-est way to freshen the air in your home, here's what you should do: Start changing your light bulbs. Yup. At this writing, special odor-killing light bulbs are just entering consumer markets. You might already be familiar with compact fluorescent bulbs, the power-saving, money-saving bulbs that last for years. The odor-killing bulbs are the same thing, except that they have a coating of titanium dioxide. When the chemical interacts with the bulb's light, it destroys the organic material in the surrounding air. This technology was developed by scientists looking for solutions to "sick building syndrome," caused by poor ventilation.

At first, you'll want to install a bulb near the cat box, in a musty basement, where smokers hang out, and any other place where odors are a particular problem. When you turn the bulb on, it takes about 10 minutes to start its odor destruction. The longer you leave

it on, the stronger the effect is. As your conventional bulbs burn out, you'll want to install titanium dioxide bulbs in every possible fixture for a whole-house odor shield. The bulbs don't perform miracles, but you will be able to scoop out cat boxes and change the litter half as often.

There are some caveats. The bulbs can do their de-stinking only when the open air can circulate past them, so they won't work in glass or plastic-enclosed light fixtures. The bulbs are a bit pricey, too. The less-costly brand, Fresh2®, is for $20 for a two-pack.

On the bright side: The odor-killing chemicals last for 3 years, and the bulbs themselves can last 7 years to 9 years. The 23-watt fluorescent bulbs also put out the same amount of light as a 100-watt incandescent bulb, meaning they provide a huge energy savings. At this writing, the bulbs are sold in some home stores, and discount stores are soon to follow. They're easy to find on the Internet.

BREAK THE MOLD

You may have seen scary reports about a creepy form of toxic mold chasing hapless residents out of their homes. Some people want to blame every disease known to humankind on mold. Others claim it's a lot of hype created by people who want to sue building contractors.

"The only reasonable place to be is in the middle somewhere," says Portnoy. The truth is, most houses have mold in them and little of it is toxic. While scientists don't know enough about how mold affects humans, there is evidence that it can trigger allergy symptoms and aggravate asthma. If nothing else, mold is worth controlling in the home because it looks and smells bad. When it gets out of hand, it can even weaken the structure of a house by digesting wood.

Mold needs two things to survive in your home. The first is food—which is the stuff your house is made of. If you remove this food, you won't have a house left. So let's move on to the second item, which is far easier to control: water. When the humidity—or moisture in the air—is above 50 percent, you're encouraging the growth of microorganisms, Portnoy says. A home's moisture problem is made worse by everyday living, including cooking, showering, other washing, and even people breathing in and out.

Many of the best ways to control humidity in your home fall into the category of one-time fixes, which means they take a little effort up front but continue to pay off far into the future:

* Central heating and air-conditioning systems typically include humidity controls, so make sure you know how to work them. Check your manual or ask a service technician.

* During warm months when you're not using an air-conditioner or if the air-conditioning doesn't dry the basement air enough, keep a dehumidifier running to pull the moisture out of the air.

* Make sure there are no leaky pipes in your house or a leaky shower stall dripping water into the basement.

* Check whether water is seeping through your basement walls. If you have a seepage problem, use a special moisture-blocking paint (available at home stores) on the interior of the concrete block. Outside, make sure all of your downspouts carry water well away from the house. If problems persist, you may need to have your yard regraded so that rainwater flows away quickly.

* Make sure your home is well ventilated. Exhaust fans that suck moist air out of bathrooms, kitchens, and laundry rooms and vent it to the outside will help control mold. If you have an older home that wasn't built with exhaust fans, installing them is a surprisingly easy job for a contractor. The next time you have remodeling, siding, roofing, or other building-type work done around the house, see if you can include exhaust fans as part of the deal.

SHOOT TO KILL Now and then, despite your best efforts at controlling moisture in your home, you're going to come face-to-face with the enemy. The minor mold incursions—a few telltale black spots on the grout in the shower or along the rim of the toilet—are easy to dispatch. Just pick up a bleach-based disinfecting cleaner (Clorox® is one brand), squirt it on, wait the prescribed amount of time, wipe, and rinse. The same cleaner will kill even moderate infestations of mold, Portnoy says, on wallboard, ceiling tile, and wood. Not only is the fungus killed, he says, but the bleach will lighten the mold stain and make it look better.

If you discover a large mold problem—say, in wallboard that has grown soft to the touch—the only solution is to remove the contaminated building material and replace it. Don't attempt this on your own, Portnoy says. The concentration of mold could be severe enough to be harmful. Ask professional home remodelers whether they handle cases like yours. Even if they don't, they'll have names of people who do. Just making the repair is not enough—make sure you figure out why the contamination happened and fix the source of the problem.

WATER, WATER EVERYWHERE

To discourage mold and dust mites, we need to keep the humidity in our homes under 50 percent. The ideal level for health and comfort is 45 percent, and 30 percent is too dry.

How the heck are we supposed to know, with any kind of precision, what the indoor humidity is? Easy: A hygrometer will tell you.

Most home hygrometers fall into one of two categories:

- **MECHANICAL.** These plastic or wood devices have a dial display and can be found for $20 or less.
- **ELECTRONIC.** These units have digital readouts, require batteries, and cost $40 or more.

These compact gizmos are easy to move around the house, but remember that they can take a couple of hours to acclimate to a new location. Don't position your hygrometer near a heat source. Hygrometers often can be purchased where indoor thermometers are sold—department stores, home stores, and hardware stores, for instance. Some hygrometers come combined with a thermometer in one unit.

If you find out that your house is too humid, adjust the humidity controls on your central air or central heating, or use a standalone dehumidifier.

OF MITES AND MEN (AND WOMEN)

The air in your home can be an invisible soup of impurities that can aggravate anybody's lungs and are a particular nuisance to people with asthma and allergies. These particles include not only mold but also dust mites, pet dander, smoke, and other airborne detritus. If you do have asthma or allergies, explore with your doctor what specific irritants you react to. Your doctor can supply more detail that's specific to your case than I can provide here. However, here are some broad strokes that any homeowner can make to yank impurities right out of the air with minimal effort.

FIGHT THE MITES Dust mites are microscopic insectlike critters that thrive on, among other things, the skin cells you leave behind in your bedding. The poop they produce is a notorious allergen. The humidity-reducing measures described earlier will help control dust mites. Wash your bedding weekly in hot water, and zip your mattress and pillows up in anti-mite covers, available in department stores and discount stores.

GET A HEAP OF HEPA FILTERS Buy high-efficiency particulate air (HEPA) filters for your furnace and vacuum cleaner. Also buy stand-alone air filtering machines to use in your living areas. HEPA filters remove from the air the kind of microscopic particles that are good at burrowing into your lungs. If you buy a HEPA filter for your furnace, consult your service folks—they may need to adjust the furnace's fan speed to accommodate the new airflow, Portnoy says. Special HEPA vacuum cleaners are available, or you can buy HEPA bags for conventional vacuum cleaners. HEPA filters need changing with a certain frequency, so pay special attention to the directions.

If you buy a stand-alone air-filtering machine, make sure you understand the unit's coverage area. Many can service no more than one typical room—and certainly not the entire house—so you may need more than one. Avoid the type of room air filters that emit ozone, which is itself a lung irritant, Portnoy says. Not all room units perform equally well, and price is not always an indicator of quality. So check consumer publications before you buy.

CHOKE OFF THE SOURCES OF POLLUTION We sometimes cling dearly to lifestyle factors that are ruining the air around us. Make the tough decisions and ban smoking from the house, quit using the fireplace, and stop lighting candles and incense. Quit using air fresheners, and don't store solvents, pesticides, and other chemicals in your home.

ALLEVIATE YOUR PET PEEVES If you're allergic to furry pets, foregoing them altogether is best. However, if you have dogs in the house, wash them weekly with a mild pet shampoo—not human shampoo and not common soap. Wash your cats, too, if you can get away with it—just wiping with a damp cloth will help. (And just in case you were thinking about it, don't spray your cat with disinfectant—believe it or not, Portnoy knows of people who have done just that.) Pet allergens and dust mites will cling to carpeting. Instead, use hard flooring and throw rugs that you can wash in hot water.

GET ALL YOUR DUCTS IN A ROW Sometimes mold will grow on old construction material left behind in ductwork, Portnoy says. Removing it is a good job for a duct-cleaning service. However, despite some of the advertising you'll see, regular duct cleaning isn't necessary.

MORE STINK STRATEGIES

Here are more ways to clear the air around your home:

USE ODOR ABSORBERS Baking soda and cat litter are two common household substances that are famous for absorbing odors in confined spaces—closets, lockers, drawers, pantries, and refrigerators, for instance. Just pour several ounces into a lidless plastic container and place the container in a hidden spot where it won't get tipped over. The baking soda or cat litter does all the work—you don't have to do anything but change it every 3 months.

KNOW YOUR SPRAYS It sounds Pollyannish to say "Read the label on your product," but it really does help to check the spray can of any odor-fighting product. If you know how the product works, you increase your chances of success in de-stinking the house. Some sprays work by killing odor-causing bacteria on surfaces, some kill bacteria suspended in the air, some trap odor molecules, and others just add a pleasing fragrance to the air (covering up— or adding to—the stink). So fit the product to the situation. In a shower stall, use a product that will kill mildew on the tile, for instance.

THIS ROBOT WILL SWEEP YOU OFF YOUR FEET

As I write this, there's a robot vacuuming my dining room. We truly have entered the age of *The Jetsons*. Only my robot isn't named Rosie and it isn't human shaped. My metal-and-plastic assistant is a cute little disc that's only 13 inches across and 4 inches high. Yes, it looks like a Foreman® grill on wheels. It's a revolutionary tool that is now available to any consumer for the price of a conventional vacuum cleaner. The Roomba® and its competitors will do for floor cleaning what the washing machine did for laundry and the dishwasher did for husbands: It takes care of a regular, necessary cleaning chore all by itself. While your robot is doing the vacuuming, you get to read a good book or go out to lunch—unless, like a number of enthusiasts, you can't resist following the little machine around the house.

The Roomba was devised by iRobot®, the same company that makes who-cares-if-they-get-killed robots for the military. While its cousins are exploring dangerous caves in Afghanistan, the homebody Roomba routs out dust and dirt in all of your living spaces. While the robot may sound intimidatingly high-tech, it's actually easy to use. It weighs no more than your purse or briefcase and has a convenient handle on top. Just turn it on, and the robot goes wheeling around the room, humming at the volume of a hair dryer set on low. The robot estimates the size of a room by seeing how far it can go in various directions without running into a wall, and then it uses math to design a cleaning pattern that will cover the entire floor.

It automatically adjusts itself to the floor surfaces it encounters—wood, tile, and carpet. (It does fine on low and medium pile, but it won't work on deep-pile carpet, shag, and such.) It can sense which parts of the floor are dirtiest and will concentrate on those areas. It also has side brushes and wall-following technology that help it clean corners and edges of a room. Because the Roomba stands just a few inches off the ground, it can vacuum where conventional vacuum cleaners can't reach—under couches, beds and chairs, for instance. Different settings instruct the robot to adjust to room sizes or even focus on one particular

CHECK YOUR ROBOT'S BREATHING

If the performance of your Roomba robotic vacuum cleaner takes a nosedive, check the filter—it may be time to replace it. You'll find an easy-access release tab for the filter on the bottom of the dirt bin, which slides out of the back of your robot part of the floor. A remote is available on some models, allowing you to turn it on from afar, direct it to specific dirty spots in a room, or pause the machine's cleaning cycle.

For recharging, the machine is connected to an electrical outlet. It can clean three average-size rooms on one charge. The newer units include a "home base" where the Roomba parks itself for recharging.

The first time I used my Roomba, I let it loose in the family room, living room, and dining room, which had been vacuumed with a conventional human-driven machine just two days before. The Roomba picked up an ounce of dust and other grime (yes, I weighed it on a postal scale)—a glob the size of my fist. This machine won't do a deep-down cleaning in your carpet—you'll still need to use a conventional vacuum cleaner for that—but it's perfect for a light cleaning every few days. Some Roomba fans say they now don't touch their conventional vacuum cleaners for months at a time.

JOIN A ROOMBA COMMUNITY

A search on the Internet will quickly lead you to an online Roomba discussion group, believe it or not. You can browse through the discussions, picking up advice about specific Roomba models, or you can get questions answered by people who have more experience than you. You'll find that a lot of owners get deeply attached to their robots—giving them names (R2D2 has been taken . . . many times over), racing them, debating what gender they are, and otherwise treating them like part of the family.

HELPING YOUR LITTLE HELPER

As independent as they are, robotic vacuums do need a little help. The human tasks are easy and fall into two categories.

READYING THE ROOM Before your Roomba goes to work, you have to prepare the room. If you're a parent, this will feel oddly like the child-proofing routine you do for babies and toddlers. The difference is, preparing for your Roomba is much easier and the stakes are much lower. It's not very likely, for example, that your vacuuming robot will sit on your cactus or stick a coat hanger into an electrical socket. Just scan the room for objects that might get pulled up into the robot's whirling brushes—plants that hang to the floor, blind cords, and lamp wires, for instance. If you have fringe on a carpet, you can tuck it under the rug temporarily. Secure the corners of small area rugs with double-sided tape. Make sure there are no objects, such as a rickety plant stand, that could be bumped over. The Roomba comes with "virtual wall" devices—little infrared flashlights—that mark off areas where you don't want the robot to go—say, through a doorless passageway.

Your Roomba may also need a little help if you have furniture that stands just a few inches off of the floor—say, the lower edge of a couch or cross-supports for an end table. Such furniture can trap your vacuuming robot. Some furniture can be raised on blocks or casters. If that's not feasible, create a physical barrier or use one of your virtual wall devices to shoo the robot away from trouble.

A DIRTY STORY
XXX
GETTING LUBRICATED

The Roomba robotic vacuum cleaner will spiff up your social life as well as your carpet. Roy Hinrichs, an Internet technology manager for a computer services company in Fort Worth, Texas, has a model with a remote control. During a social gathering in his home, Hinrichs sent his Roomba into the kitchen. His wife placed four beers on the robot's flat top. The little robot then returned to the living room and served the guests.

MAINTAINING THE MACHINE Roomba enthusiasts say some simple maintenance routines, performed after every three or four cleanings, will prevent breakdowns. In particular, you don't want long hair or other debris to get wrapped in the inner bearings or gears. To remove the robot's brushes for cleaning, all you need to do is turn the robot over, pop the wire guards off, and loosen a small Phillips-head screw. (The manual provides details.) Remove all of the hair and dirt you can find and reassemble the machine. You also can use the brush and crevice attachments on your conventional vacuum cleaner to suck dirt out of the workings of your robot. (An alternative: Blast the dirt out with compressed air.)

Assemble a small kit of the Roomba-related items you'll need frequently. These will include the following:

- A small Phillips-head screwdriver for removing the robot's brushes and cleaning inside.
- An old comb and an unbent paperclip to help extract hair and dirt from the brushes.
- Used drier sheets for dusting your robot and leaving behind an anti-static film.
- Extra filters.

These items will fit easily in a self-closing plastic bag. Store this kit in a cupboard near your Roomba.

You can buy a Roomba at discount stores, bath and kitchen stores, department stores, or on the Internet. Check how many "virtual wall" devices come with your unit—you may want to buy one or two extras. Get some extra replacement filters at the same time. You also can buy a battery

that recharges in only 2 hours, as opposed to the 12 hours it takes the standard battery. Just in case something goes wrong with your unit, buy from a retailer with a liberal return policy.

More robots could be joining your household in the near future. At this writing, the people who created Roomba were just unveiling a new floor-washing robot called Scooba®. Also on the drawing boards: machines for such tasks as washing windows and cleaning out gutters.

So there you have it—quite a collection of strategies that will make the main living areas of your home profoundly cleaner and more presentable for very little effort. Don't forget that when I suggest that you quit making the bed, install different lighting, or use a new kind of wall paint, you get to say, "No, I prefer my own approach." I'm not the God of Guilt ordering you around. If you weren't in charge, after all, it wouldn't feel like cheating.

LAUNDRY GOT YOU
OUT OF SORTS?

Jot down a quick list of the garments that you wear regularly, including clothing for work, casual situations, and outerwear. Sort your entries into two columns, one titled "Easy Care" and the other "Special Handling." Easy-Care items are those that can go into the general wash (award yourself a bonus point for each garment that's stain resistant or wrinkle free). The Special-Handling items require hand washing, delicate washing, delicate drying, or dry-cleaning. This exercise gives you a snapshot of how hard you're currently working for your wardrobe. If more than 5 percent of the clothing you regularly wear falls into the Special-Handling category, it's time to rethink the way you dress.

Unless you're a hermit, you have a valid need for the occasional piece of fine clothing, even if caring for it requires special effort. The trick is to keep such items to a minimum—nice showpieces that you mix in with a wardrobe that's predominately simple to care for.

Easy care is not the only issue. For most people, enjoyment of life is inversely proportional to the cost of the clothing you're wearing. If you spend the day in more than $500 worth of clothing, you're wearing a mental body cast—perpetually concerned about messing up those clothes and hoping your finery is creating the right illusion. That's self-induced stress. Sure, we all may enjoy the occasional silk shirt or cashmere sweater. But the stress-busting solution is to keep an eye on the balance and prevent your wardrobe from sapping too much of your physical and emotional energy.

So this is a chapter about adding "clothing sanity" to your personal agenda. In recent years, much of the working world has embraced Casual Friday—a good step. How about Casual Sunday through Saturday? Let's reserve suits for dinner at the White House. Let's dispense with men's ties altogether—an absurd garment if there ever was one. You have better things to do with money than fritter it away on fabric finery—pay for your kids' college education, pay down the mortgage, catch up on credit-card bills, or donate to charity, for instance. So let's look at some specific ways you can restore some clothing sanity to your life right now.

FABRICS FROM HELL

Some fabrics come with a guarantee: to make your life miserable. To simplify clothing care, follow the Materials on a Program (MOP) philosophy and quit adding these garments to your wardrobe. Here is Steve "The Clothing Doctor®" Boorstein's rundown of fabrics that are high-maintenance—and particularly vexing to travelers who try to haul these duds around in a suitcase. Just say no to:

- ACETATE. Difficult to iron—it shines up more quickly than chrome.
- RAYON KNIT AND SILK KNIT. Phew. Impossible to remove body odors.
- SILK. There are many grades of silk, and the cheaper variety doesn't clean well.
- SILK-LINEN BLENDS. These stain badly. Soft drink stains are particularly hard to get out.
- VELVET. Very water sensitive. "If you're a spiller, you want to stay away from most velvet," Boorstein says. Can't be ironed.

To reduce the chore of cleaning your clothes, start by making wise clothing purchases. If you consistently buy only easy-care clothing, over the months to come your laundry hassles—stains, wrinkles, delicate care, and dry cleaner trips—will be reduced by two thirds.

Once again, technology has come to our rescue. "Wrinkle-resistant clothes started out looking like people were wearing Teflon®," says Steve Boorstein, a.k.a. The Clothing Doctor, author of *The Ultimate Guide to Shopping and Caring for Clothing*. However, wrinkle- and stain-resistant fabrics have improved so much over the last decade that you can actually build an entire wardrobe out of such clothing without looking like a dork. When you stray from the wrinkle- and stain-resistant clothing, make sure you're selecting a fabric that's known for easy care. When you assemble your wardrobe with this strategy, you'll happily whistle your way through laundry day.

LABELS: THE CRUCIAL CHECKPOINT

To make sure you're getting an ideal garment for your cheat-at-cleaning wardrobe, pay careful attention to the labels on the clothing you're considering. "It's amazing how many people don't," Boorstein says—especially when they buy coats, jackets, and other outerwear. Both the hangtag dangling from the sleeve and the sewn-in fabric-care label offer valuable information about caring for a garment. Give first priority to wrinkle-resistant, stain-resistant clothing. Also, the ideal label indicates that a garment can be both machine washed and dry-cleaned. This indicates that the manufacturer has tested both approaches in the laboratory. (On the care label, the international symbol that looks like a tub full of wavy water means "wash," and a simple circle means "dry clean.")

"I believe that the care of clothing begins the moment you begin to shop," Boorstein says. "If you are a stain magnet, you really need to make sure that your clothes can be dry-cleaned *and* washed."

Oddly enough, if a label only says "machine wash" you probably can dry-clean it as well. Such labels indicate that the manufacturer tested the fabric just one way in the lab.

FAST·FORMULAS

OLD JEWELRY: RISE AND SHINE

Revive the shimmer and shine of your old costume jewelry by giving it a quick bath in white vinegar. Pour 2 inches of vinegar into a ceramic bowl and slip your jewelry into the liquid. After 2 minutes, lift the jewelry out and give any nooks and crevices a light brushing with an old toothbrush. Rinse the piece under the faucet and press it gently from both sides with a towel to dry. If you have fine jewelry that you want to clean, be careful: Many of the softer stones—such as opals, lapis lazuli, turquoise, and pearls—could be harmed by the acid in vinegar.

More testing costs the manufacturer more money, and the U.S. Federal Trade Commission requires only one laundry instruction for each garment. So if you have a "machine wash" ski jacket that picks up a greasy stain from your car door, you need to take it to the dry-cleaner's. Trying to wash out an oil-based spot at home could set the stain. (More about stains in a moment.)

If a garment's label tells you that special care is required—say, dry-cleaning only or delicate washing—a little alarm should go off in your cheat-at-cleaning head. Is this piece of clothing really worth the bother or extra expense?

Another gift from modern technology is microfiber, Boorstein says. This is a broad term for manmade cloth designed at the microscopic level to take on certain characteristics. Microfiber clothing, often a rayon and polyester blend, has an excellent drape and does not wrinkle easily.

WANT YOUR WALLET WASHED?

Empty the pockets of your clothing the moment you take them off, says Steve "The Clothing Doctor" Boorstein, who spent years as the hands-on operator of a dry-cleaning business. Otherwise, you risk having important items ruined in your washer or at the dry cleaner's. (A dry cleaner should check pockets, but sometimes he or she will miss items.)

Here are just a few items that Boorstein has found in customers' clothing in his days on the cleaning front lines: expensive jewelry, credit cards, government IDs—even a $25,000 check!

Easy-care knits, particularly cotton-polyester-Spandex® blends, also will add clothing sanity to your life, says Pamela Brown, Ph.D., a professor at the Texas Cooperative Extension at Texas A&M University. Such knits are very forgiving in the laundry room, she says—just wash, dry, remove from the dryer immediately, and hang them up to let any last wrinkles fall out.

Buy clothing in dark colors and prints, which hide stains better than light-colored clothing. Even if there's a little residual stain left after you try to remove a spot, those traces are not likely to show on dark or patterned fabric. Also, neutral colors stand up to washing over the long haul, whereas intense colors fade more quickly. If you feel drab wearing subdued colors, perk up your wardrobe through the use of accessories such as belts, scarves, and jewelry.

PLAY INSPECTOR

Once you've found the perfect garment, it's time to run off to the cash register, right? No, keep your credit card in your pocket for just 60 seconds longer. You want to be sure that the garment is really as "perfect" as it seems at first glance. Lay the clothing out on a counter or hang it up and conduct Boorstein's six-point check to make sure it's in good condition: hooks, zippers, hems, seams, snags, and buttons. Test all of the moving parts, making sure the hooks work and zippers don't catch the fabric. Make sure that the hems and seams weren't damaged by some other customer trying the clothing on. Check that all of the buttons are in place. Are there extra buttons in case you lose one?

If you're buying a finer garment—maybe a nice blouse or a sport coat—also buy a sturdy, shaped, well-fitted hanger to go with it. A high-quality, contoured hanger will keep the garment looking its best. If you use an ill-fitting hanger, you could find a bizarre dimple in the middle of the shoulder, for instance, as you dress for your big presentation. Also, avoid the clip-style hangers that have a ridge where the clip bites the fabric. These will leave impressions in the cloth. Use only the type with a smooth clasping surface.

MANAGING YOUR CLOTHES

You get your new easy-care duds home, you snip off the tags, and you set these garments free in that stream of clothing that circulates throughout your house. This is a stream that meanders from your dresser and closet, to the hamper, to the laundry room, and back again. How smoothly and easily that stream flows depends largely on you. Here are some corner-cutting clothing management techniques to help it along.

LET YOUR CLOTHES HANG OUT

When you get home from work, you want to take a little break, right? Well, your work clothes need a rest, too. So take off your shirt and pants, empty all pockets, put the clothes on hangers, and change into your jeans and T-shirt. Then hang those work clothes out in the open—on the back porch, on a doorknob, or in the bathroom, for instance.

Why? For a few good reasons. First of all, unless you got those clothes really soiled you can wear them to work two, three, or even four times before laundering. Don't blush, Boorstein says. People who study clothing use had a focus group of white-

IT'S A TIE,
NOT A BIB

If you must wear ties, spray them lightly with a stain-resistant spray such as Scotchgard®. You'll be able to mop up ketchup or wine drips without having a heart attack over the prospect of staining.

collar types—doctors, lawyers, stock-brokers, and the like—and you know what they found? These high-rolling professionals wear their dress shirts multiple times before washing them, particularly if they were wearing undershirts. So you can, too. Besides, over-cleaning your clothes is a kind of wear-and-tear in itself, so clean them only if necessary.

Here's why you hang those work clothes out in the open for at least 1 hour: Your clothes have spent the day sucking up moisture, odors, chemicals from work, and smoke from that bar where you ate lunch. Would you rather have these clothes air out—or share all of those fumes with the other clothes in your closet?

Inspect the clothes under a bright light, front and back, top and bottom. If you find grime or stains—say, around the collar, cuffs, or elbows—then they need to be laundered. Perspiration stains in particular must be washed within 24 hours. If you were to put them back into the closet for a week or two, the soil would oxidize into a permanent yellow stain. Also, give your clothes the sniff test—yes, under the arms in particular. If there's any odor, wash them. Otherwise, back into the closet they go, thus saving you some labor on washday.

STAINS MADE SIMPLE

You can find entire encyclopedias devoted to the subject of stain removal. However, if you stick to this incredibly simple rule you can't go wrong, Boorstein says: Water-based clothing stains go into your washing machine; oil-based stains go to the dry cleaner. In either case, wash (after pretreating) or dry-clean within 24 hours.

If the stain is on your own clothing, you probably have a reasonable idea of whether that stain is beer (water based) or a movie popcorn simulated-butter-like substance (oil based). However, on children's clothing it's harder to be sure what kind of stain you have, particularly if your kids' vocabulary never gets any more specific than "I don't know," "Nothing," and "Stuff." So here's how to tell water- and oil-based stains apart and how to deal with them.

WATER-BASED STAINS These almost always have a border around the perimeter that looks like a map. Examples: coffee, wine, and soft drinks. Apply a laundry pretreatment before washing (see "Stain Stopper" on p. 130, or use a commercial product). In most cases, the stain will come out fine in the wash at home.

When washing, don't forget which garments have stains—either run them through a separate wash, separate them from the other clothing in a mesh bag, or mark them with a safety pin. Remember that stains appear darker when they're wet and often are invisible, so you might not be able to tell by looking at the wet garment whether the stain has come out. Because machine drying will set the stain, let these clothes air dry

TOO EAGER TO GET IT OFF YOUR CHEST?

How many times have you seen someone in a restaurant rubbing furiously at a spot just dripped onto a blouse? Big mistake, says Steve Boorstein, author of *The Ultimate Guide to Shopping and Caring for Clothing.* It's okay to carefully blot at a stain with a fresh napkin to absorb some of the liquid. (*Blotting* means pressing down with the napkin, changing to a new part of the napkin, and pressing again.) However, never rub a stain—that could damage the fabric and ruin the color in the fibers. Just live with the splotch for the evening, and launder the blouse or take it to the dry cleaner's (depending on the type of stain) first thing in the morning.

If you're sure you have a water-based stain, blotting with a damp napkin might help, too. Club soda also is a famous emergency cure for stains (dampen a napkin with club soda and blot), but that also should not be used on oily stains or dry-clean-only clothing. It works fairly well on stains from wine, coffee, soft drinks, and some foods.

STAIN STOPPER

The earlier you get to work on a stain, the better your chances of getting it out. So when you do your evening inspection of the clothing you wore that day, here's a stain-busting formula that you can apply to spots right away. This pretreatment will hold you until laundry day. It is for water-based stains only. If you wiped french-fry grease onto your shirt, take it straight to a dry cleaner.

In a small plastic bottle, mix 1 ounce of clear (not blue or yellow tinted) dishwashing liquid with 6 ounces of water. Drip onto the stain enough of the solution to cover. Use a small brush to gently work it into the fabric. Clip a clothespin onto the stained spot so you'll remember to watch for it, and toss the garment into the hamper.

So you can grab them quickly when you need them, store the bottle, small brush, and some clothespins in a dresser drawer, in your closet, or even in the bottom of your laundry hamper.

instead—laid out flat or draped over hangers—then inspect them. If the stain is still visible on the air-dried clothing, wash again (pretreat, presoak, wash in an all-fabric bleach).

If you have a persistent stain that pretreating and laundering will not remove, take the wet (or air-dried) clothing to the dry cleaner, point out the stain, and tell them precisely what you did in an effort to remove it. Armed with this information, your dry cleaner has a better chance of getting the spot out. "It's time to be totally up front," says Boorstein, a former dry cleaner. "Full disclosure really helps."

OIL-BASED STAINS These almost always have no outline, and the stain typically has been absorbed into the fabric. Examples: egg roll grease, gravy, and hamburger drippings. Oil-based stains rarely come out in the wash, and if you do try to launder them, they will leave a blotchy remnant that will affect the color of the clothing. In most cases, it's worth the investment to dry-clean. If you insist on treating an oil-based stain at home, catch the stain fresh.

A myth-busting note: 70 percent of spot stain remover products say they remove all stains, which is impossible, Boorstein says. Tide to Go® is one of the best stain removers on the market. Its label faces up to its limitations—specifying that it is not for use on oily stains.

SOCK MATCHES MADE IN HEAVEN

The next time you're ready to buy some socks for yourself, go to your dresser, put every sock you have into a shopping bag, and donate them all to a preschool so they can make sock puppets. Yes, get rid of the seven pairs in various shades of tan, the three versions of navy blue, the green spectrum (khaki to deep forest), and the five brands of white athletic socks in various states of decay. Anything with a leprechaun, jack o' lantern, or Santa Claus on it—out it goes. Now you're ready to go to your clothing store and buy the socks that you will need to get you through only one week, says C. Lee Cawley, a professional organizer in Arlington, Virginia. For a man, depending on his lifestyle, that may be something like this: four pairs of white athletic socks for sneaker casual and five pairs of black socks for dress. If you insist, add three pairs of navy. Most important: All socks of the same color must be of the same brand and style. For women, Cawley's system isn't much different: several pairs of black trouser socks for dress and several pairs of white athletic socks for sports and sneaker casual, plus a few pairs in navy blue, gray, or brown (depending on the color of your dress trousers). Cawley also recommends limiting your pantyhose to black, nude, and—if you insist on getting complicated—gray or navy. Find a flattering, comfortable style, and buy them in bulk (usually 12 pairs at a time).

Why are we socking it to the sock drawer? Because owning 43 pairs of socks all in different styles and shades is a needlessly complicating element in your life. With Cawley's simplified sock plan, that hideous matching-up chore on laundry day will vanish. Your clothing choice when you dress in the morning will be a no-brainer. And you'll gain 2 cubic feet of space in your dresser drawer.

Photocopy, fill out, and post prominently.

A NOTE FROM
YOUR LAUNDRY FAIRY

This family's Laundry Fairy works only under specific conditions and guidelines:

1. The Laundry Fairy does not pick up or deliver.
   Laundry days are _____. Laundry delivered in your laundry basket by _____ will be washed and returned to the basket. You may pick it up by the end of the day. Please return cleaned clothes to your dresser or closet promptly.

2. At times other than those stated in No. 1, you may use the laundry equipment to wash and dry your own clothes.

3. If you have special washing instructions or clothing requiring delicate care, please write the specifics down and refer to them carefully as you do the washing yourself. See No. 2.

4. The Laundry Fairy does not iron. Ironing lessons are available by appointment.

5. The Laundry Fairy assumes you intend for her/him to wash any items left in pockets, including wallets, candy, homework, frogs, video games, and love notes. You are responsible for the results.

6. Socks delivered inside out or balled up ("stink grenades") will not be laundered.

7. To reduce wrinkles, the Laundry Fairy will smooth and fold shirts, pants, and skirts. You may fold your own underwear and match up your own socks.

Your humble servant,

The Laundry Fairy

THE PANTYHOSE SECRET: DOUBLE-BAGGING Pantyhose are a cleaning nightmare for many women. Here's Cawley's streamlined system: Buy two mesh lingerie laundry bags, one to hang on a hook in your closet and one to hold all clean pantyhose in your dresser. When you need a fresh pair, pull one out of the bag in the dresser—the color you need should be easy to grab. At the end of the day, drop them into the bag hanging in the closet. On laundry day, put the entire bag holding dirty pantyhose into the washer and then the dryer. Then slide it into your dresser and transfer the other lingerie bag to your closet.

GET A HANDLE ON SANDALS Every chance you get, wear sandals—without socks. Every day that you do represents a pair of socks you didn't have to sort, launder, dry, match up again, and deliver back to a drawer—an extra little toehold on sanity, if you will.

WASHING: LESS IS MORE

Here's welcome advice for anyone who does laundry: Do it less frequently. What most people think of as doing a normal wash actually is overwashing. Overwashing is not only a waste of time but has other undesirable effects as well: It puts more wear on your clothing, it uses up more detergent, and it increases the chances that detergent will be left in your clothes.

"Unless you have a child who has been on the playground making mud pies, most laundry just needs to be freshened," says Ingrid Johnson, a professor at the Fashion Institute of Technology in New York City. If the clothing you're going to wash has had everyday light wear—a day at the office, a shopping trip, or a day at school, for instance—use half the amount of laundry detergent that the package recommends and use the shortest, most

GREAT · GEAR

UP FRONT ABOUT WASHERS

The next time you buy a washing machine, go for a front-loading model, says Steve Boorstein, a.k.a. The Clothing Doctor. Here are the advantages of front loaders:

- They use only 5 gallons of water per load, compared to 20 gallons in a typical top loader.

- They whirl more of the water out of your clothes, so your drier has to use less energy to get them dry.

- They cause less abrasion on your clothes, meaning they'll look good longer.

- They have a larger capacity. They can easily handle big items, such as sleeping bags, that you would take to a commercial laundry otherwise.

- They generally come with more choices and flexibility in wash cycle settings.

- They're less likely to tangle up your clothing during the wash cycle.

delicate wash cycle available on your machine. "More than 90 percent of average soil comes out of most clothing within the first 2 minutes," adds Boorstein.

On the other hand, if your kids have been playing football or your spouse was knee-deep in muck in the garden, fine—give those ground-in-grubby duds the full laundry treatment: pretreating, presoaking, a full measure of detergent, and a nice long ride in the washing machine. There's just no need to give all clothing this treatment on every washday.

TIPS FOR THE LAUNDRY FAIRY

Here's advice for getting the clothes washing done with minimal effort.

TEACH YOUR KIDS RESTRAINT Children typically follow a wear-it-once philosophy and toss their clothes into the hamper whether or not they're dirty, says Brown, the Cooperative Extension prof. Train them in the quick clothing inspection techniques described earlier. Impress on them that they're lessening the household workload and protecting the environment (less use of energy and cleaning chemicals) when they wear clothing more than once.

GET THE DIRTY DUDS DELIVERED Make sure each member of the family has his or her own laundry basket for hauling clothes around. Let them know the specific day and time when laundry will be done. Anybody who wants the Laundry Fairy (that's you) to magically wash their clothes will deliver a basketful to the laundry room by that deadline. If they forget, don't wash their clothes. They won't forget again. And you won't have to forage around the house looking for clothes to wash. Photocopy "A Note from Your Laundry Fairy" (p. 132) and post it where everyone in the family will see it.

GET THE HANG OF DRYING When you're getting ready to haul your dirty clothes out of the bedroom on laundry day, open up your closet door, grab several unused hangers, and toss them into the laundry basket, too, says Cawley. Those hangers will be ready to spring into action the moment you pull a shirt or a pair of slacks out of the dryer—and hanging up dried clothing immediately means you'll keep wrinkles to a minimum. Install a hanging bar or rolling clothing rack in the laundry room just for this purpose. (Don't hang clothes on plumbing pipes running across the ceiling—you'll weaken the pipes' joints.)

DO YOUR PART Wrinkle-resistant garments can't do their wrinkle resisting all on their own—you have to help. Check the care label in the clothing. Typically, you'll be told to wash the garment in warm water, dry at a low temperature, and take it out of the dryer right away. Smooth the fabric with your hands, and hang it up. Don't expect razor-sharp creases. "It's a relaxed look," says Brown, "but it will be wrinkle free."

PUT YOUR CLOTHES INTO REVERSE Turning certain garments inside out will help protect them in the washing machine. Turn dark clothing (black jeans, for instance) inside out to reduce fading and the pick-up of lint. Also turn clothes inside out if they have anything fragile on the outside, such as hooks or zipper pulls.

FILL IT FIRST When you're starting up a load of laundry in a top-loading machine, first let the tub fill with water, then mix in

SLEIGHT OF HAND

A SHAKE PREVENTS WRINKLES

Do your clothes come out of the dryer with more wrinkles than a box of raisins? Here's an easy way to minimize wrinkles during the drying process: When you're transferring clothing from the washer to the dryer, give each garment a shake to untangle it. If you put clothes into the dryer all twisted up, they'll dry with those wrinkles immortalized in the fabric.

the additives (detergent, softeners, bleach, and such). Make sure all of the chemicals are dissolved before you put in your clothes. Giving your clothing a direct blast of cleaner is courting disaster, Boorstein says. "If you want to ruin a garment fast, put undiluted bleach directly on it."

A CURE FOR CARDBOARD CLOTHING If your garments come out of the wash feeling stiff, the detergent probably didn't wash out of the fabric well enough. To prevent this, Boorstein uses Country Save® laundry detergent. He also uses OxiClean's® Toss-n-Go™ ball, which has a very low residue and is rated least likely to remain in your clothes. In the United States, Country Save is most often found in natural-food stores and is easy to find on the Internet. OxiClean is sold in most grocery stores and on the Internet.

WASHER, WASH THYSELF Does your washing machine have bad breath? When you wash a load of clothing, billions of skin cells and other particles are left behind in the washer. To cure your machine of the resulting musty odor, run a quick wash cycle with no clothing at the end of the washday: Use the washer's briefest setting and pour in ¼ cup of bleach. An alternative: On washday, just launder your white undies as the last load, with bleach. When the cycle is done, leave the lid of the washer open until you use it again so the machine will dry out thoroughly.

For a super-deluxe cleaning of the washing machine, use a damp sponge on the under-side of the lid and the upper rim of the tub inside, particularly where water flows into the washer. Also, the holders for detergent and fabric softener can collect contaminants from clothing. Remove them and sponge them off in the sink.

WELCOME YOUR FAMILY INTO THE FOLD When you're done drying a load of laundry, slide the laundry basket up to the door of the drier, pop the door open, and drag the dry clothes into the container. If there are any shirts, skirts, or pants in the load, hang them up quickly, or smooth them out, fold them, and return them to the basket. Either way, you'll keep wrinkling to a minimum—beats the heck out of ironing them later. Just leave the socks, underwear, and such loose in the basket. Their owner can do his or her own folding and sock matching later. Leave each basket of clean clothing on the floor of the laundry room. Your family members will remember to pick them up when they run out of undies.

THE THREAT FROM "DOWN UNDER"

Speaking of undies, you might have to change your underwear. Oh, sure, you wear a fresh pair every day. What I mean is, some kinds of undies don't lend themselves to good sanitation. If you have the wrong kind, toss them out.

Here's why. Charles Gerba, Ph.D., a microbiologist at the University of Arizona in Tucson, got curious about sanitation issues involving the laundering of used underwear. His tests showed that the typical pair of used underwear contains a tenth of a gram of fecal matter, also known by the scientific term *poop*. That's equivalent in weight to one quarter of a peanut, he says. And that's a heck of a lot of nasty bacteria.

What happens when you wash dirty underwear with other clothing? Yes, some of the bacteria get washed down the drain. However, a significant amount of bacteria are evenly distributed among all of the clothing in that wash load—enough bacteria to sicken the person handling these clothes. The typical warm wash and the typical drying time do not kill them all.

A DIRTY STORY

GERM OF AN IDEA

Usually, you'd have to wonder about a middle-aged man who would buy used underwear from the young people he knows. In fact, when Charles Gerba, Ph.D., carted home a pile of his students' dirty undies, his wife exclaimed, "Oh my God, what are you doing?"

It was all in the interest of science. Gerba, a microbiologist at the University of Arizona in Tucson, was studying the transfer of bacteria from underwear during the laundry cycle. He acquired his test underwear from the most readily available source—the student body, if you'll pardon the term.

Aside from the lessons of science, Gerba made an interesting discovery: "If you ever have to cut up underwear, a pizza cutter works great," he says.

He's also happy to have done a good turn for his young protégés. "I know all my students have new underwear—I ground up the old ones," he says.

The solution? Wash all of your underwear separately from other clothing in hot water with detergent and bleach, and then dry them for 45 minutes, Gerba says. That will kill the bacteria and make handling your laundry safe. Unfortunately, some of the more fashionable and decorative kinds of underwear call for washing in cold water with no bleach. Throw them away or convert them to cleaning rags, and then buy some undies that will stand up to the rigors of sanitation. You might have to give up on the idea of looking like a fashion plate in your skivvies.

HANDY HAND WASHING

Hand washing bras, lingerie, and other fragile items is a breeze as long as you follow the number 1 rule: Don't put much effort into it. "There's no reason to overwash clothing that doesn't require it," Boorstein says. Many sweaters can be hand washed too, but make sure you take cashmere to a dry cleaner. Here's his easy, no-fuss approach to hand washing:

- ✳ Run cold water in the sink until it's 4 inches deep.
- ✳ Add delicate detergent according to the package directions.
- ✳ Let the garment soak for 2 minutes.
- ✳ Swish the garment around with your hands.

* Drain the water, then refill with fresh water to rinse.
* Hang the garment up to dry.

Here's an alternative to hand washing sweaters that will save you some time and effort:

* Wash the sweater in your washing machine using cold water and the shortest, gentlest cycle.
* Spin the sweater for 10 minutes in the dryer, set on the lowest setting.
* Lay the sweater flat on a towel to finish drying.

TABLECLOTHS: TABLE THAT IDEA

The plates and glasses are tucked away into the dishwasher, the leftovers are packed into the fridge, the serving dishes are drying in the sink-side rack. Ahhh, you've just about recovered from your holiday feast—except for that battle-scarred white tablecloth. Ready to wrestle it into the laundry room?

Don't even bother, says Boorstein. The simplest—and really the only—cure for a feast-stained tablecloth in the United States is to drop it off at the dry cleaner's immediately. The reason is a sad tale of lagging technology. American washing machines are no match for the typical tablecloth stains—wine, gravy, butter, and wax, for instance. The water in typical American machines reaches only 110° to 120°F, but removing these stains requires water near the boiling point, at least 190°F. European washers have long had heating elements that boost the water temperature to the proper level. Front-loading washers with heating elements are a new item in the American market.

If you do try to launder that tablecloth at home without the temperature boost, here's what will happen: You'll wash the cloth. In the bad light in your laundry room, you'll fail to notice the faint, blotchy remnant of the stains. You'll fold the tablecloth and stick it into a drawer, where those remnant stains will oxidize. When the next big feast day comes, you'll pull the tablecloth out again, and then you'll stomp around the room ranting about the stains that magically appeared. "Every household in America has a tablecloth with yellow or brown stains," Boorstein says.

So skip right over all of that angst, and make a quick trip to the dry cleaner part of your postfeast cleanup routine.

Now That They're Clean . . .

Sorting, folding, ironing, and storage. You work so hard for those darned clothes that they ought to cut you a paycheck every week. No matter. There are plenty of ways to cheat at the postwashing stage.

TAKING TURNS IS LOADS EASIER

Washing your family's clothing isn't labor intensive. The tough part comes before and after washing—sorting all of the stinky clothing into color-coded piles and then, after washing, "unsorting" them back into each family member's laundry basket. A weekly wash for a family of four could easily involve two loads of dark clothing, two loads of colors, two loads of lights, a load of towels, and a load of whites. How could you possibly cheat on laundering an inhibiting mountain of clothes like that?

Easy: The strategy is to peel the sorting out of the process. Just don't wash everyone's clothing on the same day. Pick a few different days of the week to wash clothes, and wash only one family member's clothing on each of those days. On Monday, launder your teenager Julie's clothes. On Tuesday, it's your spouse's turn, and so on. This makes the laundry sorting incredibly simple—each washday, all clothing comes out of and goes back into only one basket. You'll be able to get it all done in just a couple of loads. If the Laundry Fairy in your house is so astoundingly generous as to provide delivery service, each day's clothing needs to go to only one person's bedroom rather than several locations around the house.

YOU GOTTA KNOW HOW TO FOLD 'EM

If you've played air guitar, then you're going to have no problem playing "air laundress." After washing and drying, do you fold each garment by laying it flat on a surface and then meticulously folding each sleeve or plant leg into place? Switch to this in-the-air quick-fold technique, and you'll shave 20 minutes off of your laundry duty. Here's how it's done:

* Pick up a newly dried shirt with its front facing you. Hold it with a hand in the middle of each shoulder.

* With the shirt still dangling there in the air, turn your hands so that you fold each sleeve behind the shirt (along with a few inches of shoulder).

* Lower the shirt into the laundry basket so that the bottom half of the shirt hits the surface face down.

* Drop the top half of the shirt onto the bottom half, thus folding the shirt horizontally across the middle.

Practice this technique, and soon you'll be able to fold a shirt, T-shirt, or sweater in 1 second flat. Adapt the process to pants, skirts, and any other clothing—basically, you want to set a garment down only once, in its final resting place. No, this approach isn't as precise as folding on a flat surface. Any family member who complains, however, gets to do his or her own folding.

CURES FOR SHRINKING AND STRETCHING

It's a magic trick: Your teenager's sweater goes into the washer a perfect fit but it comes out the right size for her 10-year-old sister. Here are Boorstein's easy methods for handling clothing shrinkage and the reverse malady—stretching.

If there's a chance the sweater you're washing will shrink, whip out a tape measure and mark down its dimensions (height, width, sleeve length, and such). When the sweater comes out of the wash, lay it out still damp over a dry white towel on top of the washing machine or on a laundry table. Check the dimensions you recorded. If the sweater shrank, gently "reblock" the sweater by pulling easily with your fingers until it's back to its original size. Let it dry lying right there.

If you have a problem with your jeans shrinking, fold them the long way while they're still moist—so the legs are flat against each other. Pull at the top and bottom ends to stretch the jeans into shape. If the waist comes out of the washer too snug, wrap the waist (still damp) around the edge of the laundry table and pull. You can do the same for the tight collar of a dress shirt.

There's also an easy cure for stretched-out sweaters. Sweaters typically stretch in the neck, cuffs, or waist when you wear them, and stretching also can happen when a long garment gets wrapped around the agitator in the clothes washer. Just wash the sweater as usual. After washing, lay it out still damp on a dry, white towel. Then pinch, push, and squish the fabric together. The sweater will dry in that "tightened" condition and stay that way (until you stretch it out again).

To prevent stretching, pilling, and other damage, always wash your sweaters or long, stretchable garments in a mesh laundry bag, available in fabric stores. An alternative: Wash the garment

in a pillowcase held closed with a thick rubber band.

PITFALLS OF PRESSING

You can measure your cheat-at-cleaning success by how often you have to fire up the iron. Every other day? You are a slave to your wardrobe. Once a month? Not bad. Forgot where your iron is? Now, *that's* living!

If you insist on using an iron now and then—maybe you just can't live without a 100 percent cotton dress shirt—then you'll want to know how to keep the chore to a minimum. Here are the most common ironing mistakes, Boorstein says:

LEAKING ALL OVER YOUR CLOTHES It's usually the older irons that leak, so get one that won't. Read the manual and make sure you know how to operate that steam button. You might be flooding the steam chamber by pressing it too much.

SPITTING IMPURITIES ONTO YOUR CLOTHES Use distilled water in your iron unless your model is specifically designed for tap water. Otherwise, the steam function may spray staining minerals all over that blouse.

PRESSING TOO HOT When you're ironing, more is not better—you'll ruin the fabric. Use the heat setting that matches the fabric you're ironing.

GREAT · GEAR

A MINI BOARD FOR EASY IRONING

The wide-open parts of a blouse are a breeze to iron. It's the sleeves and nooks and crannies of the garment that take up most of your time. The job will go more smoothly if you use a sleeve board—basically a mini ironing board—to press those hard-to-reach spots. When you iron sleeves on a sleeve board, you no longer have to press the sleeves flat, creating those long creases. Sleeve boards are typically about 20 inches long and a few inches wide. Look for them wherever you buy ironing products or do a search on the Internet.

SOME IRONCLAD RULES

Here are other ways to satisfy your pressing needs with a minimum amount of effort.

WASH YOUR FACE The face of the iron, that is. Using a clean iron will reduce the odds of staining and yellowing. Put some baking soda into a bowl and add enough water to make a paste. Wipe the paste onto your iron's face (while it's cool) with a damp cloth. Turn the cloth over, and wipe the paste off. You also can buy iron-cleaning products in supermarkets and discount stores.

STEAM POWERED

How would you like to eliminate just about all of your ironing chores? Steve "The Clothing Doctor" Boorstein swears by his wrinkle-busting garment steamer. Let's say you have a crowded closet and a skirt came out wrinkled, or a knit shirt sat unused for months and now there are fold lines down the front. Just hang the garment on a knob, turn on the steamer, shoosh the offending spot, and the wrinkle will be gone in seconds. You get to skip the entire process of setting up your ironing board and pressing.

Boorstein swears by the Jiffy® Steamer brand, which offers a home model and a smaller travel version. "I now actually pack in a very different way—I never worry about wrinkles," he says.

MAKE SURE YOU'RE COVERED Impurities and laundry products such as starch can build up on your ironing board and transfer to the clothes you think you're cleaning. Boorstein's simple solution: Use two ironing board covers. When one gets soiled, wash it and use the spare in the meantime.

GO EASY ON THE TRIGGER When you spray clothes for ironing, use a minimum of water. If you soak the garment you're ironing, you're more likely to sop up impurities from the ironing board cover.

BUY A BEEFY BOARD A high-quality ironing board can make all the difference in the quality of your ironing. The problem is that a cheap ironing board will sometimes bend in the middle, causing the iron to dig into the fabric you're ironing and cause a mark. Buy an ironing board that's so sturdy it feels as if you could sit on it.

USE AN INTERMEDIARY Certain fabrics are sensitive to high heat and can turn shiny if you set the iron too hot. This applies in particular to acetate, gabardine, certain twills, and polished cotton. Use a muslin pressing cloth between the iron and the garment to protect such fragile fabrics. Or just turn the garment inside out and press the reverse side. Never iron velvet—period.

DO IT DAMP Pull your blouse out of the dryer while it's still slightly damp and iron it right away. This way, your blouse won't have to recover from dryer-induced wrinkles. "That will cut down on 50 percent of your ironing time," Boorstein says.

REMOTE STORAGE

It's the rare person who feels as if he or she had enough closet space. As ruthless as you might be about weeding out unused or unnecessary garments in your wardrobe, it seems like there's never enough rail space for everything you want to hang. You already know the basic solution: Use other locations as temporary storage. You might rotate seasonal items in and out of your bedroom closet, you might fold up clothes and store them in containers, or you might permanently park infrequently used garments (an evening gown or tuxedo) in some remote part of the house. But there's more to storing clothing than just shifting them from one spot to another. There are precautions to take and a few myths to be busted, says Boorstein.

CLEAN IT FIRST Before you store any clothing, first make sure every item has been washed or dry cleaned. Always empty the pockets.

BAG THE BAG Always remove the dry cleaning bag—the clothes need to breathe. Leave those little paper shoulder covers on—they'll keep some dust off.

TUCK THEM IN When you're storing clothes in a remote closet, line the garments up on a hanging rail and throw a clean, unbleached sheet over them all. This will keep dust at bay and protect them from fading. (Yes, even low light will have some effect over time.)

FORGET THE MOTHBALLS Avoid mothballs. They leak, you can't remove their odor from clothing, and they're toxic.

SURRENDER THE CEDAR You know that time-honored notion that cedar products protect your stored clothes? "It's a fallacy," says Boorstein. To protect your clothes, the cedar must have a strong, pungent odor, but 99 percent of cedar chests and drawers in use do not do any good because they've lost that scent. Restoring that odor requires reconditioning of the wood, which no one is going to bother with.

HIRE IT OUT If you use a dry cleaner's storage service, they will clean and store clothing in a climate-controlled facility. Before you do this, however, make a computerized list of all of your items (year after year, you'll be able to edit the list on your computer). Check your home insurance to make sure that it covers off-premises storage.

The bottom line is that laundry, like dishwashing, is a cleaning duty that just never quits. It accounts for a large percentage of the time you spend cleaning every week, and as with many large tasks there is no single way to cut corners. The cheating lies in multiple techniques that whittle away at this monster that has taken over your life. You might not even realize how onerous the laundry has become until you feel the relief that comes with wise buying, clever management, and savvy dirt busting. It's time for a little laundry revolution in your home. So get going—you have nothing to lose but your chains . . . and your stains.

YOUR DESK AND WORK AREAS: WINNING THE PAPER CHASE

K eeping an orderly home office is not just about aesthetics. Your personal and professional reputation is on the line. If your home office is dysfunctional, you miss appointments, pay bills late, spend hours looking for lost documents, and offend clients and colleagues.

On the other hand, nobody wants to be a slave to a filing cabinet and an anal-retentive office system. My computer doesn't have enough disk space to hold all of the school-marmish rules for how to run a home office. Chances are you've read an article or two about how your home office "ought" to be set up and run—complex systems, baffling software, and, just to make us all laugh, a spotless desk at the end of each day. Your eyes cross, you tell yourself you'd rather stick your hand in a meat grinder, and you continue with your comfortably slobbish office habits.

Well, you're going to feel better after you meet Jeff Zbar of Coral Springs, Florida. On the workday we talked, he had a house full of kids. If that weren't distraction enough, there were no fewer than 20 personal, nonbusiness items vying for his attention in his home office (child art, a poster, quotes, his drum kit, and more). He gets a clear view of his desktop only every few weeks. He's a great believer in stacks of barely organized paper. He stacks magazines on the floor. And the most delicious thing: He's a successful consultant on the subject of home offices.

"I'm organized in my disorganization," says Zbar, who does business as The Chief Home Officer. "I fear people who have no paper on their desks."

In this chapter, then, we'll find out more about how Zbar organizes his own office. I'll share some easy, low-maintenance, no-slave-work techniques from other sources as well. If you have an office job outside of the home, you're going to find plenty of useful advice that applies there, too. Home offices are a highly individual thing, Zbar emphasizes, and it's crucial that you find a system that clicks for you.

"Tip number one is make your own rules," he says. If they work, fine. If not, have the wisdom to change them. Now, that's the *How to Cheat at Cleaning* spirit!

CLUTTER: HOW'S YOUR DESK STACK UP?

Zbar has a few core strategies that keep his home office ticking efficiently. Stacks, for instance. While stacks of paper are a no-no to organizational purists, Zbar manages swimmingly with a few stacks of paper on his desktop, all of them pertaining to current or near-future concerns. While an outsider might find no rhyme or reason to the content of each one, Zbar is confident he can find any paper he wants within seconds—and that's all that counts.

One stack plays a pivotal role in getting excess paper "out of my face," he says—the stack of papers that are ready to be filed. When a document has served its immediate purpose but must be kept for the future, onto the stack it goes. Every few weeks, Zbar spends 45 minutes on a Saturday morning putting these papers into their proper files. Similarly, every few weeks he totally clears off his desk—typically when he has finished a large project for a client. Cleaning his desk more often would interfere with his work, so to heck with conventional wisdom.

EASY-DOES-IT FILING

This brings us to filing systems. Zbar is a fan of the simple, no-frills approach—just a filing cabinet and oodles of file folders. ("There's a reason file folders come in boxes of 100," he says.) There's no need for computer-printed file labels or other fancy trappings. Start your filing system with broad categories. As needed, subdivide large topics into subtopics. For instance, "Insurance" might have subfolders of "Insurance—Car," "Insurance—Home," and "Insurance—Medical."

Don't make your filing system any more complicated than it needs to be. Consider how often you need to retrieve each kind of document. For instance, if you almost never need to retrieve old utility bills, you probably can use one folder for the power, water, phone, and cable bills. Making separate folders for each utility just makes the system more laborious to maintain.

Make maximum use of the vertical space around you. To keep surfaces in your office clear, mount everything possible on the wall—telephone, paper organizer, and lamps, for instance. Put tools, reference books, and computer peripherals on shelves above and around your desk. Use stacking trays or vertical files near your desk for sorting papers that are related to current projects.

Another area where simplicity is best: technology. "I'm not a believer in using technology that goes beyond what you need," Zbar says. Cutting-edge computerized gizmos, complex software, and other extravagances will sap not only your money but also your time and mental energy as you learn how to make them work. Heed the saying "The leading edge will make you bleed." Ask yourself, "Does this widget really make me more efficient and therefore more productive?"

There's a flip side to the issue of office technology: Make sure that the machines you do keep in the office are up to date and in good repair. Equipment that is obsolete, broken, or works only marginally will become more and more of a drag on efficiency as time passes.

CUT OFF CLUTTER AT THE SOURCE

Here are more ways to make sure clutter never gets a chance to smother your home office.

STAMP OUT MAIL MESS When you pull mail out of the mailbox, sort it right away so you don't have to handle it twice. Zbar has an outside trash receptacle near his garage where he drops all junk mail (after tearing it in half) so it doesn't even get into the house. He drops all bills into the top right-hand drawer of his desk, where he stores his checkbook and other family finance materials. Mail for his wife goes onto her desk. Magazines go onto a special "read-soon" stack in his office. Whatever you do, don't plop the mail down unsorted onto a desk or counter—it will just get absorbed into a monster clutter pile, never to be seen again.

HOME OFFICE WISH LIST

Your office is already stocked with paperclips, scissors, tape, and envelopes. Here's a list of less common office gizmos that professional organizers say will help you reduce clutter, save time, and save effort.

- **USB HUB.** USB connections are the standard for PC gear these days, but many PC towers offer only two or three ports—sometimes in a hard-to-reach place. A USB hub places several ports right on your desktop, meaning you'll never run out of room for USB headphones, flash drive storage devices, and such.

- **WIRE CHASE.** For easier office cleaning and an orderly look, bundle that tangle of cables behind your desk into a wire chase, a channel or tube that will hold them together. Also, use plastic zip ties (available at home improvement stores) to bind up excess lengths of wire behind your computer.

- **SMALL TOOL KIT.** Instead of running to the toolbox every time you need to make a little repair, keep a small tool kit in a desk drawer. Include a tiny screwdriver, a tiny Phillips screwdriver, needle-nose pliers, and other tools you think you'll need.

- **COMBINED SCANNER-PRINTER-COPIER-FAX.** Consolidate your computer equipment as much as possible. Why have a separate scanner, printer, copier, and fax machine, when there are single units that will handle all of those tasks? This will save you several square feet of counter or shelf space.

- **LABELER.** If you need to worry about appearances for professional reasons, or if you just like sharp-looking labels, there are machines that produce durable, laminated labels for shelves, bins, binders, and envelopes.

- **SHREDDER.** How many cubic feet of bank statements, receipts, cancelled checks, ancient tax forms, medical papers, and other documents are you holding onto just because you're afraid, for security reasons, to throw them away? You need a paper shredder at your desk. Some models will also shred credit cards and CDs.

OPTICAL MOUSE: CASE CLOSED

With a simple equipment change, you can eliminate a cleaning issue and computer hassle from your life forever. The conventional mechanical computer mouse, the kind with a roller ball on the underside, has an annoying flaw. It likes to pick up dust and collect it inside the mechanism. Slowly, your mouse loses agility until you find yourself struggling just to move that little computer arrow from one side of the screen to the other. You have to disassemble the mouse, pluck out the gray fuzz with tweezers, and put it back together again. A better approach: The newer optical mouse. Instead of a roller, it uses light sensors to detect movement. It's a more accurate system, and no dust gets inside the case of your mouse, so it stays squeaky clean.

CORRAL THOSE ITTY-BITTY DOCUMENTS Receipts and credit card slips from everyday purchases present a quandary. They're official documents that prove you made particular purchases from particular stores. But how often do you really need to retrieve an old receipt? Two or three times a year? Here's a simple, no-effort way to keep your receipts organized in case you need them. Each time you make a purchase, put the receipt in your pocket. When you get home, put any receipt that you might need for taxes into a file in your office. Put receipts for high-priced items such as jewelry and major appliances into your home insurance file or a fireproof box. Throw away any receipts for minor incidental purchases— a candy bar, dental floss, or cellophane tape. All other receipts go into an easy-access shoebox or small drawer. Place the receipts in their container in chronological order (just plop the most recent receipts at the front). If you need to locate one of these receipts in a month or so, you'll have a rough idea of where to find it. When your storage container gets full, pull a handful of receipts from the back of the drawer. These will be a few years old and entirely useless by now. Run them through a shredder or drop them into a box labeled "Destroy" and toss them into a campfire.

DON'T FILE IT, GOOGLE™ IT Yes, stuffing papers into file folders will get them off your desk and keep your work area clean and neat. It's better, however, to throw away every piece of paper you possibly can, says Zbar. Before you put printouts of research into a folder, ask yourself: "Can I easily find similar material on the Internet any time I want?" If the answer is yes, then recycle those papers instead of filing them.

MAXIMUM STORAGE, ZERO SPACE Speaking of computers, conduct as much of your daily business on your computer as possible, and store your documents there electronically. Resist the temptation to print out documents that you can easily retrieve from orderly computer files. This keeps paper clutter to a minimum in your office. Word processing and e-mail programs typically allow you to make unlimited storage folders on your computer. As a memory aid, use an electronic folder system that follows the same logic as the hard-copy folders you keep.

QUIT WRITING CHECKS Sign up with your bank for electronic bill paying—it's simpler and faster than using checks, and it doesn't require stamps, envelopes, or a trip to the mailbox.

GET DRASTIC WITH PLASTIC Open your wallet and cut up all but three or four of the most useful and versatile credit cards you have. The fewer services you use, the less "mindshare" you have to devote to running your daily life, Zbar explains. Zbar limits himself to four cards: a debit card and credit card for the family, and a debit card and credit card for business. What's in your wallet?

TAKE CARE OF BUSINESS No matter how casual you might be about the order of your home office, there will be certain materials that need quick and careful filing. For instance, if you work out of your home office—as a telecommuter or a home-based business—slide all project-related papers into a labeled folder the very moment you're done with them. You want those papers at your fingertips if your client or boss calls to talk shop. If you want a sane approach to home cleaning, you have to focus on priorities—and your livelihood is a big one. Here are some other papers that you should put in their proper "homes" the moment they arrive—don't set them down in a pile: checks to be cashed, bills, tax documents, and car registration papers.

COMPUTERS: KEEPING A CLEAN MACHINE

In just about anybody's home office these days there is, front and center, a viewing screen attached by cable to a large whirring box. You need to keep your home computer "clean" in two senses: Keeping it dust free will help ensure that it runs properly, but it's even more important that you keep your computer clean digitally—that is, free from viruses, adware, spyware, unused programs, and other threats.

If you at all depend on the proper functioning of your home computer, here's my number 1, cheating-est, angst- and labor-saving recommendation: Develop a relationship with a professional computer technician—someone who makes house calls routinely to fix and maintain computers. Such a technician offers a level of service that cannot be found over the "help line" at a mail-order computer company or at the repair counter of a computer retail store. Find a technician who has several years of professional experience in troubleshooting and repairing home computers (the teenager down the block won't do). A talented technician will save you wheelbarrow loads of heartache. But don't wait for disaster—make an appointment with your new tech now to review your system even if it's humming along smoothly. Then he or she will know you and your computer whenever your hard drive melts down. Don't bother with a repair company that asks you to take your computer in and leave it for a few days.

Once you have a professional computer tech programmed into your speed-dial, you may be ready for level 2 of computer "cleaning," which also is pretty darned easy. The following concise lists will help you protect, maintain, and physically clean your home machine. If you hit all of these points, you'll be light-years ahead of the typical computer user. A tip of the hat goes out to advisers Joe Grant, owner, and Alexander Barco, technician, of Computer Medic in Dublin, Pennsylvania.

DEFENSE AGAINST INVASION

Think of the Internet as one big digital mud pit. The more you cruise through it, particularly with high-speed connections, the greater your chance of getting your system dirty—that is, infected with harmful, secretly delivered programs. Here's how to prevent that.

INSTALL A WALL Firewall protection will make your computer resistant to a wide variety of viruses (destructive programs), adware (hidden advertising programs), and spyware (hidden programs that provide data about you to outsiders). A firewall can come in one of two forms—hardware (a box that stands between your computer and your Internet connection) or software.

INOCULATE YOUR COMPUTER Buy special software for your computer that will detect and destroy viruses, adware, and

E-MAIL: SUBJECT TO REVISION

Home office consultant Jeff Zbar, of Coral Springs, Florida, is a big believer in using focused, descriptive subject lines in all e-mails. Why obsess about a detail like that? Because when you file important e-mails into various electronic folders, you want to be able to retrieve that information easily. The quickest way to do that is by scanning the subject lines. If your subject lines are vague, you have to go on a scavenger hunt, opening up one e-mail after another until you find what you want.

What if someone sends you an e-mail with no subject line at all, or a subject line that gives no clue to its content? Zbar simply forwards the e-mail to himself with a rewritten subject line, then files it. There are other options, depending on the e-mail program you use. For instance, in Outlook® and Eudora®, you can call up an e-mail, change the subject line, and save it again. G-mail allows you to attach labels to your e-mails and conduct a search on those labels later.

TAKE SPAM OFF
THE MENU

Wish you could close down the pipeline that funnels unsolicited phone calls, junk mail, and e-mail spam into your life every day? There's no total solution, but in the United States adding your name to lists at two Internet sites will help:

- **THE FEDERAL TRADE COMMISSION.** Visit www.donotcall.gov and put your telephone number on the do-not-call list. Most telemarketers (some are exempt) will have a month to quit calling you.

- **THE DIRECT MARKETING ASSOCIATION.** Visit www.dmaconsumers.org, and click your way to the consumer assistance information. Add your name to the lists of people who don't want unsolicited telephone, mail, and e-mail marketing pitches. Some companies (not all) use these lists to purge their rosters. Over the following months, you should notice a marked drop-off in junk solicitations. Depending on how you register, you may encounter small processing fees or have to print out a form, fill it out, and mail it in. But if this reduces the marketing noise that assaults you every day, it will be worth it.

spyware. You'll probably need more than one program. This technology changes rapidly, so ask an experienced computer technician to recommend the best brands. (Don't just talk to the salesperson at the computer store.) Many programs allow you to schedule an automatic, full-system sweep. Do this at least weekly. To make sure your computer will recognize the most current threats, see that your software is updated frequently.

AVOID INTERNET "HOT" SPOTS X-rated Web sites often are brimming with hidden adware and spyware ready to leap onto your computer uninvited. Avoid such sites altogether. I'm not being judgmental —just presenting the bare facts.

BEWARE "FREE" DOWNLOADS Don't download third-party software, programming that is unbranded or branded with a name that's unfamiliar to you. Such programs are not as well tested as the famous-name software and may not be compatible with other software you rely on. Programming that you download from top software makers probably won't harm your computer, but read every word of the fine print first.

HANDLE ATTACHMENTS WITH CARE Whenever someone sends you a file attached to e-mail, do not open the file straight off the e-mail. Save the file to your disk so your protective scanning programs can check it over first. Delete all junk e-mail immediately.

NO-BRAINER MAINTENANCE

Some simple habits will keep your computer whirring happily and protect all of the good work you have stored on the hard drive. Because systems and software vary and change, I can't provide step-by-step details. However, the HELP function on your computer will provide easy instructions or your computer tech can walk you through it. Enter reminders for these procedures into your electronic calendar. Many of the following details apply specifically to the Windows® operating system and Microsoft℠ software because they're overwhelmingly the most commonly used. If you're a Mac® user, talk to your tech about the REBUILD YOUR DESKTOP, REPAIR PERMISSIONS, and DISK FIRST AID functions, as well as other routine maintenance.

BACK UP YOUR FILES This involves the mass copying of all the personal files you have on your hard drive to a large-capacity storage device that's outside of your computer—for instance, a CD, a zip disk, or an external hard drive. If your computer's hard drive crashes, your files might not be retrievable. With backup files, you can resume business immediately on another computer until you get your main rig repaired. Back up your files at least weekly—daily if you generate lots of data.

BABY YOUR HARD DRIVE Run the CHECK DISK function on your computer every 6 months. This will examine your hard drive and patch up any physical problems. Also, run the DISK DEFRAG-MENTER program, which will rearrange the data on your hard drive so that it functions most smoothly.

UPDATE THE OPERATING SYSTEM When you hook up to the Internet, Windows should alert you when updates are available for the operating system. You also can get updates manually through the TOOLS menu on your Web browser. These updates are important for the smooth running and security of your computer.

PURGE INTERNET FILES Once a month, go to the TOOLS menu on your browser and click on INTERNET OPTIONS. Delete the temporary Internet files (also called the "cache") and cookies, which can bog down your computer and present security problems.

PURGE YOUR PROGRAMS Every 6 months, review your computer for programs you no longer use, and delete them. (Go to the CONTROL PANEL, which has a program deletion function.) Heaping unused programs onto your computer will slow the system down.

A PHYSICAL CLEANING, TOO

They have yet to invent software that will clean the physical dirt from your computer. Fortunately, it's almost as easy as hitting a DELETE button—although there are a couple of important cautions.

WIPE OUT DUST To remove dust from the exterior of your computer casing and a conventional screen, all you need to do is wipe it down with a lightly dampened sponge (water only) or paper towel. Never spray any fluid directly onto your computer—drips could damage the electronics. Use a disposable duster if you prefer. The newer LCD screens are plastic, not glass, so remember that they are particularly delicate. Use only a damp, soft, lint-free cleaning cloth on such screens. Wipe them with a gentle side-to-side motion, not in circles.

GO UNDER COVER I know, going inside your computer box is scary. But dust can build up inside, causing it to overheat. This will lead to expensive repairs. So once a year, unplug the machine and open up the case of your computer. Computer covers are held on in various ways, often by two screws you have to loosen on the back. On a typical computer tower, you usually want to remove the cover on the left side of the box (as you face its front). Put the brush attachment on your vacuum cleaner and suck the dust out, being careful not to bonk any of the electronics or loosen any connections. Then snap the cover back into place. Never blow inside your computer, either with your mouth or with compressed air. That could force dust into the workings of your CD drive or other devices, where it will do damage. While you have the vacuum all set up with the dust attachment, turn your keyboard upside down and give it a gentle shake. Vacuum up all of the potato chip crumbs that fall out, then give the keyboard itself a once-over with the brush.

MIND GAMES

Let's set aside hardware and filing cabinets for a moment. Clutter control in your home office depends a lot on the mental side of managing your workspace, too. Here's a look at how office layout, decision-making, and planning will lend some sanity to your desktop. A little brainpower expended up front will pay off handsomely in time and energy saved.

FIND THE RIGHT FREQUENCY Are the tools and papers you need for your day-in and day-out work easy to grab, use, and return to their homes? If they are, then the objects around you will naturally settle into order rather than accumulate in a chaotic

A CLUTTER-FREE DESK IN 5 MINUTES

You say the clutter on your desk is beyond repair? You would happily adopt clutter-free work habits—but that rolling heap of paper in your work area is so inhibiting that you never summon the courage to start? Or perhaps the problem is even more urgent—say, a client is dropping by within minutes, and your reputation will be ruined when she sees that desk?

Don't worry, we're going to have that desk cleaned off in 5 minutes. Just follow these steps:

1. Get two large cardboard boxes. Label the first box "To Be Filed," the second "My Desktop" and add the date.

2. Set a timer or just glance at your watch while you work. Spend 10 seconds grabbing up any papers from current projects and throwing them into a folder. Now take 3 minutes to move all the papers on your desk into one of the two boxes. Don't stop to think—you have time only to move papers by the handful. If you come across intact file folders or other materials that obviously belong in your

filing cabinet, put them into the first box. That's probably 5 percent of the heap. All the other papers get shoveled into the second box.

3. Park the "To Be Filed" box near the filing cabinet. Put the "My Desktop" box into a short-term storage spot—the corner of the office, a closet, or the basement.

4. Quickly pick through any remaining junk on your desk. Throw the usable supplies into your supply drawer. Throw away the broken buttons, candy wrappers, ancient sticky notes, and dead bugs.

5. Wipe down the desk with a damp sponge or disposable wipe.

Now you can make a fresh start at your desk. If you ever think you need one of those old papers, you know right where they are. They're no more or less organized than they ever were—they're just not in your way any more. If a year passes and you haven't opened the "My Desktop" box, throw it out. Even if you never reform your work habits, you now have a crude system for de-cluttering the desk once a year.

heap. Here's an easy way to plan your workspace for maximum efficiency: Sit in your desk chair and look at all the items in your work area. Rearrange your possessions so they radiate away from you in terms of how urgent they are. The things you use several times a day should be within quick-and-easy grasp. Items you need two or three times a day should be within reach. Items you need two or three times a week should be no more than a step or two away from your chair. Items you need two or three times a month should be on the periphery.

To make frequently used items accessible, put extra effort into creating close-at-hand storage and making the best use of space:

* Some sleek-and-modern desks have no desk drawers at all, notes Elizabeth Hagen, a professional organizer in Sioux Falls, South Dakota. In that instance, substitute a stand-alone rolling file unit.

* Go vertical: Use shelves and stacking trays, and mount everything possible onto the nearest wall.

* The next time you buy a computer monitor, get a flat-screen model rather than one of the conventional, bulky, dust-magnet CRTs.

* Buy electronics that combine multiple functions into one unit rather than buying separate devices. This way, only one machine has to be within reach rather than several.

PUSH-BUTTON-EASY CLUTTER CONTROL

In a typical computer game, you have a mission to accomplish (say, make the world safe for humankind) and a barrage of unexpected matters to cope with along the way (that bug-eyed alien crawling out of a manhole). You have an array of tools and strategies available for wending your way through the game.

Working in your home office can be much like that. You have a main mission (often, keeping your financial empire intact) and myriad incidental problems to cope with along the way (responding to an e-mail from your bug-eyed accountant). As with the computer game, if you ignore the barrage of matters competing for your attention, they'll mount up and eventually eat you alive. Indecision about the papers on your desk will not only bury your work space in an unsightly heap but will reduce your efficiency as a worker, tarnish your reputation when you don't deal with matters promptly, and cost you business from people you've offended through neglect.

There's a simple secret for vanquishing desktop clutter forever. It's as easy as pushing a button every time a problem, large or small, presents itself. Think about it, says Hagen: All of the input that crosses your desk will come in one of five forms: paper, voice mail, e-mail, verbal requests (Mommy, I need a Halloween costume—tomorrow!), and things you think of on your own. For any of these matters, make a split-second decision—all you have to do is choose from one of five easy responses. In videogame terms, think of the following as the five buttons you can push every time input enters your life. Write these five terms down and post them in a prominent place at your desk:

Toss it Just throw the item away—shred it, recycle it, or delete it. Ask yourself about the worst-case scenario: What's the worst that could happen if I throw this out and I discover that I need it later? If you can live with those consequences, toss it. Learn to love this response. Remember: Willingness to throw stuff out is one of the prime *How to Cheat at Cleaning* virtues.

Delegate it That is, pass the matter off to someone else. Pick the right person, clarify what you want done, verify that the other person understands (get him or her to repeat the instructions), get the other person's agreement to participate, and then specify a completion date.

Act on it If acting on this matter will take 2 minutes or less, just do it immediately.

File it for follow-up If acting on this matter will take more than 2 minutes, put it in your to-be-done-later file, or on your calendar, under the appropriate date. (More on simple to-be-done-later files in a moment.) The beauty of filing for follow-up is that you don't have to perform the task immediately—just commit to when you will do it.

File it for future reference When must-keep papers fall into your lap (tax materials, insurance papers, and medical records), store them in your standard office files. However, go easy on this approach, says Hagen: 80 percent of what we file we never look at again.

Notice that when you use one of these five responses, no papers are allowed to settle onto your desk. If you train yourself to immediately push one of these five buttons for every bit of input that crosses your desk, your work area will never be cluttered, colleagues will be impressed by your organization, and you won't ever have to apologize for having misplaced important materials. You will rule the world.

A DIRTY STORY
XXX

A LITTLE LIGHT READING

While it's an easy factor to ignore, light will make a big difference in the function of your office. Not only does light tend to lift your spirits, but the lack of light will render parts of your office unusable. You won't realize it, but you will confine yourself to the parts of the room where there's good illumination. Or you'll abandon your poorly lit office altogether and work elsewhere in the house—spreading chaos and clutter.

To make sure your entire office functions smoothly, install lighting that's strong and evenly distributed about the room, says New York City architect Evan Galen.

HOW SHARP IS YOUR SECOND BRAIN?

Every adult needs some kind of system—some kind of "second brain"—for reminding herself or himself what to do when, and for locating the relevant materials associated with it. At the simplest level, such a system might entail a calendar you can jot notes onto (or the computerized equivalent), a to-do list you keep on your desk, and a set of vertical files kept within easy reach for current active projects. If you have a homegrown system such as this and it works for you, stick to it. However, if you're exhibiting symptoms of disorganization—heaps of paper clutter, commitments forgotten, or paperwork lost—it's time to adopt one that is more orderly.

Hagen recommends an incredibly easy to-be-done-later reminder system that she calls "core files." When you're making rapid-fire, instantaneous decisions about all of the niggley problems that confront you daily, now and then you say, "I'll deal with this later." Maybe your mother called asking you to mail a photograph from last summer's vacation or perhaps a client sent an e-mail asking you to revise a report and return it within 2 weeks. If you jot a note to yourself and just plop it onto your desk, you'll lose the reminder and forget to follow through. However, Hagen's core files make sure that you get reminded to perform each task you have committed to and that you have all of the relevant papers on hand.

Drop by an office-supply store and pick up a couple boxes of hanging file folders. You will need an easy-access place to park these files—preferably a desk drawer. If you don't have one, buy a plastic file box that has the ridges to support hanging files and put it near your desk. Label one set of folders for each day of the month, 1 through 31. Label 12 more folders January through December. Finally, label a separate folder for each person that you interact with regularly—your spouse, each child, an assistant, or a colleague, for instance.

If you have to fly to Dubuque, Iowa, on the 18th of the current month, drop all of the relevant paperwork—ticket information, itinerary, and contact information—into the folder labeled "18." If the trip isn't until next April, file the material in the "April" folder. If your assistant is making the trip instead of you, put the papers into the folder with his or her name on it.

Now for retrieving the information you have socked away. At the beginning of each day, open up the folder that corresponds to the day of the month and check the tasks that you have committed yourself to. Everything you need should be right there. At the end of each month, open up the next month's folder and sort any materials and reminders that you find into the appropriately numbered folders. Whenever you encounter the people you have made the special name-labeled folders for, hand them the contents of their folders.

"This system will never crash on you," Hagen says. "Make it a part of your life, and you will have a clutter-free desk!"

THE GREAT OUTDOORS:
DECKS, SIDEWALKS, DRIVEWAYS, GUTTERS, SIDING, WINDOWS, AND ENTRYWAYS

It's a tough, damaging, grimy environment beyond the walls of your home. A lot of the outdoors is just plain *made* of dirt, so it's surprising that anything you leave unsheltered ever gets clean at all. Complicating matters are harsh sunlight, temperature extremes, air pollution, vegetation, wind, rain, snow, ice—and, of course, bird poop. Because many of the things we leave exposed to these elements need special protection—decks and sidewalks, for instance—cleaning projects often expand into waterproofing projects, too.

Cleaning the exterior of your house, the walking surfaces, and your outdoor possessions is a big, big job, one that can take over your life if you let it. Unless you cheat. Which means buying easy-care or no-care products to begin with; using cutting-edge, labor-saving tools; and following your priorities and forgetting about the rest. Or just saying to heck with it and moving into an apartment. This last option may of course seem rather drastic, so let's focus just on the cheating.

Inside the house, the hardest-working, most indispensable cleaning tool is undoubtedly the vacuum cleaner. For outside of the house, there's an equally powerful, multitalented appliance, although it's not yet as ubiquitous as the Hoover® in your closet: It's the pressure washer. This device will take an hour's work done "the hard way"—say, cleaning the garage floor with a mop—and reduce the task to a few minutes. You'll wonder why you went so long without one.

For the uninitiated, pressure washers squirt a super-fast stream of water out of a metal wand, knocking grime off surfaces that normally would require diligent scrubbing. Most pressure washers have devices that allow you to add detergent to the spray when desired. Light duties for a pressure washer include cleaning garden tools, lawn mowers, patio furniture, automobiles, and grills. Heavy duties include spiffing up siding, decks, driveways, and sidewalks. Because they do their cleaning through high pressure and not by the sheer volume of water, they actually use 80 percent less water than your garden hose.

BUY THE RIGHT PRESSURE WASHER

Before you open your wallet to buy one, first consider what you want to clean with a pressure washer. (Your rake and trowels after a gardening session? The 800 square feet of patio?) Then consider how those needs match up with the two basic types:

ELECTRIC. Electric pressure washers tend to have less power—1,300 to 1,700 pounds per square inch (psi). They're great for cleaning items with smaller surface areas. Although they tend to cost a little less, remember that you're going to find yourself tethered to an outlet.

THE GREAT OUTDOORS

GAS-POWERED. Gas-powered washers can have twice the pressure of electric models and can make short work of large surface areas. But although they clean faster, they're also louder.

Wielding all of this power also means you have to take precautions. You don't want to dig a groove into your deck or chip paint off your car—which can happen if you're not careful. So when you start to clean, hold the tip of the wand at least 2 feet from the object you're cleaning and slowly move closer if you need the extra punch. Protect your body, too. At a minimum, always wear goggles and shoes when you use a pressure washer, says Jon Hoch, who sells the devices online through his company Pressure Washers Direct, based in Romeoville, Illinois—preferably boots with rubber soles. As odd as it sounds, it's easy to cut your foot with a pressure washer if you're not wearing shoes. Sandals and flip-flops are a no-no.

If you want to save money on a pressure washer, Hoch says, two strategies will cut the cost in half: Either buy a reconditioned model, or split the cost with a neighbor and take turns using it.

Here are some more tips for using your pressure washer, whether you're cleaning the deck, siding, patio furniture, grill, garage floor, or driveway:

GET THE RIGHT CLEANER Pressure washers can do a lot of cleaning with pure water alone, but mixing in detergent makes them even more effective. Make sure the label on your detergent says it's okay for pressure washers.

LET THE SUDS SIT When using your pressure washer to apply detergent, turn off the washer and let the cleaner sit for 10 minutes before you rinse. This gives the detergent time to do its dirt-loosening job before it gets washed away in the rinse water.

TAKE CAREFUL AIM Don't go overboard with that blast of water. You don't want to force water into a light fixture or vent, or behind the siding on your house.

DECKING DECISIONS

If you're building a new deck, the kind of material you choose will have a big effect on the time you spend cleaning and maintaining it. Here are some things you'll want to know:

- PLASTIC DECKING. If low maintenance is your priority, this is the way to go. It's easy to clean and doesn't tend to fade. *Drawback:* As much as the manufacturer may try to create a wood look, you're gonna know it's plastic. Visit a showroom or home show that has a deck built of the material you're considering buying, and decide whether it's for you.

- COMPOSITE DECKING. These materials are usually made of 50 percent wood flour (ground-up wood, finer than sawdust) and 50 percent plastic. You get what you pay for. The higher-quality versions do a decent job of simulating natural wood. Those with a higher plastic content will last longer. Composite decking is easy to clean and doesn't require waterproofing, although you might want to use deck stain to help maintain the color. Note,

however, that this decking can bow in high heat, and mildew can degrade the wood flour component, weakening the boards.

- PRESSURE-TREATED LUMBER. The most common pressure-treated lumber for decking is either yellow pine or Douglas fir, depending on where you live. Of the natural woods, these are the easiest to care for. They come treated to resist rot and termites, but they still need protection from water damage. (Some decking now comes with pretreated waterproofing, but make sure it's labeled that way if you're going to skip the sealing process.)

- EXOTIC WOODS. Cedar, redwood, and tropical hardwoods require more care because you need to take extra steps to restore their color during your periodic cleaning and resealing. Consider these an AILment (Anxiety-Inducing Luxury).

BUY A BRUSH Pick up a siding brush that slips onto the end of your spraying wand. The light scrubbing action will help loosen dirt when you clean your siding.

HIDE YOUR MISTAKES First apply your pressure washer to an inconspicuous part of the object you're cleaning to make sure it won't be damaged.

THE WIND AT YOUR FINGERTIPS

Leaf blowers are another versatile outdoor power tool that make quick work of cleaning tasks, in particular blasting leaves, twigs, and dirt off your deck, patio, porch, sidewalk, and driveway. If you spend a miserable amount of time behind a push broom outside—or if you ought to, but you don't have time for it—take the leap into power blowing. Unless you have an enormous yard or you have to work far from a power outlet, the electric models are the way to go—they're less expensive, lighter, and less hassle to operate. Many models have a vacuum option, allowing you to suck leaves and debris into a bag. Some even mulch leaves and dump them into a trash can. The smaller, handheld blowers are fine for most homeowners, but if you need an enormous amount of power, check out the backpack or wheel-around models.

Be aware that these machines are noisy—loud enough that ear protection is a good idea. Be considerate of your neighbors, who might not want to be blasted out of bed at 7 A.M. on a Saturday. Many communities are so up in arms about the noise created by incessant leaf blowers that they're passing laws against their use.

In fact, Lance Walheim, a garden expert for Bayer® Advanced lawn care and pest control products, dislikes the noise of his own leaf blower so much that he uses a different power tool for getting his leaves off the lawn quickly: He puts the grass-clipping bag onto his lawn mower and mows the leaves up wherever they lie—no blowing, no raking. Mulching mowers do a particularly good job of grinding up leaves. The shredded leaves are compact, so they're easier to handle and fit into fewer lawn bags. You also can pour the shredded leaves onto your garden as mulch or onto your compost pile to rot.

THE SURFACES UNDERFOOT

What separates us from nature? Well, roofs and walls to be sure. But also the hard surfaces we create outside to keep our feet and vehicles from sinking into the muck. Our decks, patios, sidewalks, and driveways are extremely durable, built to withstand years of abuse from rain, snow, pollution, boots, tires, and children. Happily, the wind and rain often do a stellar job of keeping these surfaces free of dust and grass trimmings. Once a month or so, you might be inspired to take a 2-minute tour around the house with a leaf blower to give them a gale-force cleaning. (Use a push broom if you have tons of excess time and need the aerobic exercise.)

Over the years, however, these manmade surfaces grow dingy from embedded dirt that no power blower or broom bristle can budge. The solution is a special kind of cleaning involving tools and chemicals that do deep-down dirt removal. Once that's done, there's generally another step: adding a sealant that will help the surface shrug off damaging water and dirt in the future. Yes, it's a tad involved, but the alternative is to let these outside surfaces crumble into disrepair—taking you to a whole new level of expensive hassles.

Fortunately, cutting-edge tools and materials are steadily making the cleaning and protection of these outside surfaces easier. Here's how.

SIZING UP YOUR DECK

We associate decks with leisure living, so it would be a shame if such an amenity actually made your life miserable. Let's look at how we can clean and maintain our decks while keeping the work to a minimum.

Day-in and day-out cleaning of a deck is a simple matter— a quick sweep with a push broom or a squirt from the garden hose will usually do. But in the case of a wooden deck, every few years, and in some cases every year (depending on materials), you need to do a thorough, deep-down cleaning or it will quickly deteriorate and fall apart. The job can be broken down into three phases, but none of them is difficult if you have the right equipment and know-how:

1. **ASSESSMENT.** Figure out whether your deck needs resealing, consider what material it's made of, and

---

THREE STEPS FOR PROTECTING THOSE PLANTS

When you spray cleaner or waterproofing onto your deck, it's hard to keep some of that spray from splashing onto the nearby landscaping. Here's the easy way to protect your lawn and other plantings:

1. Before you treat your deck, take the spray nozzle on your garden hose and thoroughly water down all nearby plants.
2. Cover your plants with plastic. Plastic painters' drop cloths work well for this.
3. After cleaning or waterproofing your deck, remove the plastic and thoroughly spray the area again to dilute any cleaner that made it onto the ground.

THE LOW-MAINTENANCE LANDSCAPE

Many a cheat-at-cleaning enthusiast has stared out at the lawn and had a thought like this: "I should just landscape the entire yard and eliminate mowing forever." That's an admirable idea—but be careful. The cleanup and care of some landscaping features are actually more trouble than a few extra square feet of conventional grass, says Alissa Shanley, a landscape and garden designer in Denver, Colorado.

We asked Shanley how she would design a yard if low cleaning and maintenance were the top priorities.

- PICK PATIOS. A patio made of concrete, or a combination of flagstone and concrete, needs much less maintenance than a wooden deck.

- COVER UP. A permanent awning or roof over your patio will drastically reduce cleaning-oriented tasks. Dirt and debris will be deflected onto the lawn. Your outdoor furniture will be protected, so you'll be able to quit hauling it in and out of the weather. And once your patio is permanently "made in the shade," you'll have no further need for that annoying patio umbrella that keeps blowing over.

- BRANCH INTO EVERGREENS. Evergreen trees are low maintenance, because they don't drop any leaves you'll have to clean up. Many people cover their yards with conventional leaf-bearing trees, forgetting what a massive job the raking will be in the fall.

- FOREGO THE FLOWERS. Converting lawn into beds for shrubs and flowers is a mistake. Those plantings will require trimming and weeding. Flowers need deadheading so they'll continue to bloom, plus cutting down at the end of the season. If you're trying to reduce maintenance, this trade-off is not worth it. "I say let's do grass and hire your neighbor kid to cut it—that's the least maintenance if you want something growing," Shanley says.

- FORGET THE FOUNTAIN. People often tell themselves, "I'll just install a fishpond or fountain in my yard—and I'll never have to touch it!" Wrong, says Shanley. Fountains and ponds require constant cleaning. If you fall behind on cleaning them, leaves and debris will blow in, clog the system, and burn out the pump.

decide what you want your deck to look like once you've treated it.

2. **Cleaning.** A good cleaning will remove embedded dirt, mildew, and that gray tinge that wood develops when it's left out in the weather.

3. **Sealing.** Apply waterproofing to wooden decks periodically to protect them from water damage. If you want to stain your deck, use a waterproof seal that stains at the same time so you're not adding extra steps to the process.

If you're reading this book, you certainly don't want to deep clean and reseal your deck unless it's absolutely necessary. Victoria Scarborough, Ph.D., director of research and development for Thompson's Water Seal®, says this is the simplest way to decide if your deck's old waterproofing is still intact: On a dry day, pour a glass of water onto your deck's surface and watch what happens. If the water is absorbed into the wood and creates a darkened splotch, it's time to reseal the wood. If the water runs off or beads up, go find something else to worry about—your deck is fine.

TIME FOR PRESSURE CLEANING

If your deck needs resealing, there are a couple of issues to consider before you run off to your home-improvement store. What kind of sealer and stain are currently on your deck? This could affect what cleaner you use. Also, what do you want your deck to look like? Its natural wood color? Slightly stained to a new tone? An opaque color that still shows the wood grain? Your answer will affect what kind of sealer you buy.

Cleaning your deck will remove dirt, mildew, algae, weathered-gray wood cells, and remnants of old waterproofing—all of which can interfere with your new sealant. The certified *How to Cheat at Cleaning* method for removing this stuff from your deck is to apply deck cleaner using your high-pressure sprayer. (Remember, you ran out and bought one after reading about them earlier in this chapter.) A high-pressure sprayer is powerful enough to gouge a groove into your deck's wood, so take it easy. Scarborough recommends a setting of no more than 1,200 psi. Follow these steps:

* First use the pressure washer to rinse any surface grime off the deck.

* Add cleaner to your pressure washer, spray it onto the wood, and let it sit for several minutes, according to the package directions.

* Switch to plain water again and put on a narrow spraying tip (but not the narrowest). Sweep the spray back and forth across the wood to loosen the embedded dirt and rinse off the detergent.

If you don't have a high-pressure sprayer, your backup plan is to apply the cleaner with a pump-style sprayer, which also is available at your home-improvement store. In this case, you'll need to scrub the cleaner in with a synthetic broom before rinsing.

Not just any old cleaner will do for this job. Make sure your cleaner is specifically made for decks. Deck cleaners come in several intensities, too, so find one that's a match for your situation. They will fall into these categories:

GENERAL CLEANER. For removing dirt, mildew, and old oil-based sealant.

HEAVY-DUTY CLEANER. Removes not only dirt and mildew but also old water-based sealant and tints.

CLEANER AND BRIGHTENER. Helps preserve the color of redwood and cedar.

STAIN REMOVER. Strips away the paint-like solid stain.

NOW SEAL THE DEAL

Once your deck is clean, it needs a fresh coat of waterproofing. Most sealants tell you to let your deck dry for 2 days or 3 days after cleaning. If you shop around, however, you can find newer sealants that can be applied as little as 2 hours after cleaning— meaning you can now clean and waterproof your deck all in the same day. Check what weather conditions are required—you'll probably need clear skies for the next day or two and temperatures between 50° and 90°F.

Keep in mind that the clear sealants generally have to be reapplied after 1 or 2 years, whereas the more opaque stains last 2 or 3 years. Whichever waterproofing you decide on, heed this advice: Wave good-bye forever to oil-based sealants and their messy clean-up requirements. Modern water-based sealants are as good or better than their stinky oil-based counterparts and can be cleaned up with simple soap and water.

There are a number of easy ways to apply waterproofing. A pump-up sprayer will do the job most quickly. (If you're using a tint, make sure the spraying mechanism can handle heavier pigments.) Rollers and paint pads will do the job fast, too—use an extension pole so you don't have to bend over and ruin your back. Use a conventional paintbrush to apply the sealant to the odd spaces around railings where pads and rollers can't reach. If the weather is ideal for drying, you'll probably be able to walk on your deck after 24 hours—check the directions.

SIDEWALKS AND DRIVEWAYS

Plenty of people go a lifetime without doing anything more to care for concrete than sweeping it or squirting it with the garden hose. There are good reasons to go a step further once every several years, however. Concrete has lots of pores, says Scarborough, which are "great traps for just about every icky, dirty thing that there is outside." This includes oil, grease, sap, and mildew.

A thorough cleaning of the sidewalk can add a "like new" touch to the appearance of your house. And adding sealer to the concrete has several benefits: Your sidewalk will slough off dirt and stains, so it will look clean with little further maintenance; it will repel water, preventing the damage that freezing and thawing causes; and it will make shoveling in the winter easier, because snow and ice will not be able to reach into the pores of the concrete and grip the surface.

Cleaning concrete is much like cleaning your deck. Buy a cleaner specifically made for concrete. Apply it according to the directions and let it sit for 15 minutes or so. If you have a high-pressure sprayer, use it to rinse and loosen any stubborn dirt. Otherwise, scrub with a stiff-bristled brush and rinse with the garden hose.

When the concrete is clean, apply the waterproofing with a pump-up sprayer or a roller. Look for a high-quality sealant that will last for several years.

If you have a single oil spot on a sidewalk or driveway—say, from a leaky automobile—you can find a number of driveway-cleaning products at your home-improvement store. But this tried-and-true home remedy might be all you need: Sprinkle cheap cat litter onto the spot, stand on the litter, and grind it in with your shoe, then let it sit. Cat litter is highly absorbent and will suck up the oil. After 3 hours, just sweep up the litter.

What if you have an asphalt driveway? Manufacturers say spreading driveway sealant on asphalt every few years will prolong its life, protecting it from weather and UV rays. Skeptics say that driveway sealer adds little protection. But all agree on two things: It's particularly important to patch any cracks in your driveway with a crack-filler product so water doesn't undermine your driveway, and follow up with a sealant to provide a nice cosmetic touch, at the very least.

THE HOUSE ITSELF

Here's where we talk about housecleaning in the literal sense—actually cleaning the outside of the house. Your house has a number of systems designed to keep the outside on the outside, including the roof, gutters, downspouts, siding, and windows. In the course of performing this service, they get grimy with airborne particles, speckled with sap, festooned with leaves and twigs, and spotted by birds with uncanny aim. These systems work best and look their best when they're cleaned periodically. So let's see how they can be spiffed up with the minimum amount of effort. And just to make sure none of this outside grunge gets *inside* your house, we'll discuss how you can easily set up a mudroom as a last line of defense.

PUT YOUR MIND IN THE GUTTER

A lot of home maintenance involves making sure water goes where you want it to and nowhere else. Outside, this means keeping your rain gutters and downspouts clean. If your gutters are clogged, rainwater will back up and rot the fascia board of your house (the board under your roof line that gutters are attached to). Water from overflowing gutters can pool around the base of your house, too, causing the foundation to shift and the basement to flood. Dripping gutters also will dig a mini-trench in your yard and ruin landscaping.

If you want to make gutter cleaning a minimal task, there's a preventive secret I'll bet you never thought of: Give the roof a quick sweeping. Sweeping the refuse away while it's on the roof is a lot easier than digging it out of a clogged gutter later on. Walheim's approach is the easiest of all—get up there with a leaf blower and blast all the debris off your roof in just a few seconds. If you don't have a leaf blower, it's still a quick job with a push broom. Chase away all the bark, twigs, leaves, and dirt once or twice a year, particularly in the fall after the leaves have dropped from the surrounding trees, says Alisa LeSueur, executive director of the American Association of Rain Carrying System Installation Specialists, based in San Antonio, Texas. (If you decorate your house with Christmas lights, get that task done at the same time.) If you have trees that also shed debris in the spring, sweep the roof then, as well. If you're sweeping, use a dustpan to collect the debris, or shove it off the edge of the roof with enough force that it doesn't fall into the gutter. Two cautions: Make sure you're not sweeping debris onto someone's head down below and do

WHEN YOUR GUTTER RUNNETH OVER

How do you know you have clogged rain gutters? Easy: The next time it rains, grab an umbrella, go outside, and take a look at the bottom end of your downspout. If there's little water coming out, you know the rain is going somewhere else—and that can't be good news for your house, says Alisa LeSueur, executive director of the American Association of Rain Carrying System Installation Specialists. Also look up: Is water dripping off the sides of your gutter? That's another sign that your gutter is dammed up inside.

THE GREAT OUTDOORS

THE INS AND OUTS OF
GUTTER COVERS

A number of systems will help keep debris out of your home's rain gutters. These covers will save you some gutter-cleaning work, but none of them is totally trouble free, says Alisa LeSueur, executive director of the American Association of Rain Carrying System Installation Specialists.

With solid hood-style gutter covers, water flows over the solid hood, through a slot on the outside of the cover, and into the gutter. One style requires that you slide the inside edge under your roof shingles. Another requires that you lower the gutter. In one particularly expensive model, the gutter and hood are all one piece.

Screen-style covers are another option, but these are more likely to trap debris between the roof's edge and the gutter cover, requiring some rooftop sweeping.

Either style of cover can be overwhelmed by heavy rain, causing water to sheet off the side of the gutter.

Questions to ask your salesperson:

✿ Will I have to reposition my current gutter to accommodate this cover?

✿ Are special brackets required for installation?

✿ Will this cover work with my style and size of gutter?

✿ Will this work with my style of roof shingle?

roof work only when there's a buddy around to call for help if you fall.

Once the roof is swept, attack the gutters. Walheim says a leaf blower set on the vacuum setting will make quick work of a leafy gutter. Or slip on a glove and work your way down the gutter, pulling out any leaves and twigs and tossing them to the ground.

What if you've ignored the issue of rainwater for years, and now your gutter and downspout are choked with a few inches of slimy, composting leaves? Your neglect has made the job harder, but a few tricks will get you through. As mentioned earlier, sweep the roof, if possible, so there's no more debris rolling toward your gutters. Then take the following steps, in order.

REMOVE AN ELBOW If your downspout is clogged, you might be able to loosen up the leaves and twigs inside with your garden hose. Get on a ladder, stick the hose into the top hole of the downspout, and turn the hose on full blast. If that doesn't work, loosen the screws on the middle elbow joint, the most likely culprit. (There usually are three elbow joints on a down-spout—one at the top, a second one high up, and one at the bottom.) Turn your head to the side so you don't get a face full of water, remove the joint, and shake the leaves out. If the bottom elbow of the downspout is clogged, too, put on a work glove and reach in to pull the debris out. Or bend a wire coat hanger so that you can poke the hook into the elbow and yank the junk out.

Sometimes the top elbow joint is glued into place, so don't try to force that one off. Leave the downspout disassembled until the gutter above it is clean—there's no sense in clogging up the downspout again with debris from above. When you do reassemble the downspout, make sure that the "male" end of each piece is pointing down so that water is always directed inside the downspout, LeSueur says.

START SHOVELING Decide whether you want to tackle the job from the rooftop or from a ladder. Cleaning from the rooftop

A SIDING SOLUTION

Usually, the only cleaning your aluminum or vinyl siding will need is a squirt of regular water from your garden hose or high-pressure sprayer. But for built-up grime, you might need the help of a dirt-busting cleaner and the aid of a siding brush. Apply the following solution and rinse immediately, says Alisa LeSueur, executive director of the American Association of Rain Carrying System Installation Specialists.

- ⅓ cup laundry detergent
- ⅔ cup trisodium phosphate
- 1 quart household bleach
- 3 quarts water

eliminates the hassle of moving your ladder around, but you have to be comfortable working on your hands and knees at the edge of the roof. Also, decide where you want to put the muck that's pulled from your gutter. Throwing it onto the ground might be fine, or you may prefer dropping it into a bucket or onto a tarp.

If there are a few inches of rotting leaves and sticks in your gutter, you need some kind of mini-shovel to get it clean. Gutter-scooping tools are available at your home-improvement store. Buy the kind with an extension handle so you don't have to move your ladder as often. Or you can improvise—dig the debris out with a putty knife, a wooden paint stirrer, or a plastic motor oil bottle cut in half.

MAKE SOME RAIN Put your downspout back together and give it a dry run (or should we say "wet run"?). Rinse the gutter and downspout inside and out. Make sure that water squirted into the gutter is now running unimpeded out the bottom of the downspout. If a seam on your gutter is leaking, buy a caulking-style tube of gutter sealant at your home-improvement store and follow the package directions for filling the crack on the inside of the gutter.

There—that's as bad as the job will ever get. Now raise your right hand and take an oath to check your gutters at least every year and more often if there are trees near your house.

PUT YOUR WINDOWS TO WORK

If your house has a lot of windows, you've probably found yourself outside on a ladder with a bucket and squeegee, thinking, "Some day, windows will clean their own darned selves." That day is here, actually.

As improbable as it sounds to many people, homeowners really can buy windows that will clean themselves (on the outside, anyway). The key is a thin coating of titanium dioxide on the glass, which is activated by sunlight and speeds the breakdown of the organic material that can collect on windows—sap, resin, bird poop, and such. These windows also sheet off water quickly, so inorganic stuff like road dust washes away readily each time it rains—or with a quick squirt of the garden hose.

"I never clean them in my home—I never touch them," says Chris Barry, an engineer for Pilkington®, a Toledo, Ohio, company that makes self-cleaning windows.

As you might expect, replacement windows with self-cleaning glass cost more than conventional ones. But wouldn't you pay more if it meant you never had to wash windows on the outside of your house again? Now, I'm not suggesting that you tear out your current windows just to save a few hours' labor. However, if you're building an addition onto your home or if you're replacing old windows anyway, self-cleaning glass would be worth the investment. To get these windows for your home, do an Internet search on the term "self cleaning glass" and check out the manufacturers' Web sites, which will list window dealers they work with in your area.

FAST·FORMULAS

YES, IT DOES WINDOWS

Here's an easy, dirt-busting formula for cleaning the exterior of your home's windows, from Tom Gustin, product manager for Merry Maids℠ cleaning service. Mix it up in your window-washing bucket:

- 2 gallons of warm water
- a small squirt of dishwashing liquid
- ½ cup of either ammonia or vinegar

Okay, I know what you're thinking: It could be years before you install self-cleaning windows, and you want to know how to cheat at window cleaning right now. No problem. Stop in at your home-improvement store or hardware store and pick up a bottle of outdoor window cleaner, the kind that attaches to your hose. Hook the bottle up according to the directions. You'll be told to rinse the windows, spray the cleaner on, let it sit for several seconds, and rinse again. That's it—no squeegee, no drying rag, no bucket, no ladder. The cleaner is formulated to run off, streak-free. You can even spray the cleaner through screens onto windows, and it will easily reach windows on the second floor.

Do you prefer the hands-on, up close and personal approach to cleaning windows? There are plenty of cheat-at-cleaning shortcuts even for squeegee-and-bucket fans. Tom Gustin, product manager for Merry Maids cleaning service in Memphis, Tennessee, recommends that you start with a squeegee that has a long sponge on the flip side and a socket where you can twist in an extension pole when needed. You also need a bucket that's wide enough to accommodate the squeegee, plus a dry micro-fiber cleaning cloth (this high-tech material draws up dirt rather than smearing it around like conventional cotton). Mix up the dirt-cutting window cleaner you'll find in "Yes, It Does Windows" on p. 183.

Now take the squeegee in your dominant hand and the cloth in the other and follow this quick procedure for each window:

1. Dip the squeegee into the cleaning solution and rub its sponge side over the entire surface of the window.

2. Draw the blade of the squeegee across the top of the window in one horizontal strip. Wipe the blade with the cloth.

3. Working from one side of the window to the other, wipe the remaining cleaning solution off the window in overlapping vertical strips. For each swipe you take, start

the squeegee at the top in the dry part of the window and draw down. Wipe the blade after each swipe.

4. Wipe the cloth over the edges of the glass to dry.

CONDUCT A SPOT CHECK

Now and then you'll run across spots, stains, or grime on your windows that are too tough for conventional cleaning. Here are handy tools that will help you dispatch those stubborn blemishes with a mere flick of the hand.

MILD ABRASIVE CLEANER A gentle household abrasive cleaner does wonders for those milky mineral deposits that can form when your lawn sprinkler splashes the glass.

ACID CLEANER Mild acid also will make quick work of splotchy glass. Look for a household cleaner that contains citric acid or use plain ol' white vinegar.

SCRUBBER SPONGE Carry a white scrubber sponge with you (the white ones are the least abrasive) to rub out stubborn spots on the outside of your windows.

RAZOR SCRAPER Also carry in your pocket a razor scraper, the kind with a retractable blade. This tool will eliminate the toughest stains, such as paint drops and hardened bird droppings. First wet the stain for lubrication, then slide the razor into the spot from the side. Move the razor in one direction only (sawing it back and forth could scratch the glass).

Two cautions: If you have self-cleaning windows described earlier, make sure you read the manufacturer's directions for care. You could damage the self-cleaning coating with aggressive spot cleaning. Also, while you might be tempted to use a pressure washer for cleaning your windows outside, Hoch doesn't recommend that. The pressure could loosen the putty that holds the glass in place.

MUDROOMS: NO DIRT MAY PASS

A mudroom is a dirt-catching zone that stands between your home and the great outdoors. If you stop the dirt there, you won't have to chase it all over the house with a mop or vacuum cleaner. Even if the designer of your house didn't bless you with an officially designated mudroom, equip your most commonly used entrance with the gear and systems that will keep bucket loads of grime out of your house. Depending on the traffic pattern in your home, your mudroom might be an enclosed porch, the entrance from the garage, or even the front entryway.

"A great deal of the dirt that comes into the house comes in on shoes," says Sarah Smock, a spokesperson for the Merry Maids cleaning service company. So the way you outfit your mudroom will depend a lot on what the residents of your house have wrapped around their feet as they come and go. Are you a single professional who wears nothing but leather soles? Everyday mats might be all you need. Got a family of six with kids ranging from 5 years to 17 years old? You need major dirt insurance.

MATS ARE A MUST Large, strong mats for wiping feet are your home's first and best defense against dirt. Put one just outside the mudroom door and just inside. Depending on your setup, natural fiber mats might work just fine, but remember that if your mats are directly exposed to the weather, synthetic materials will hold up better.

BE READY TO BRUSH Leave a stiff-bristled scrub brush outside your mudroom door to use on shoes and boots that are so messy that mats won't suffice. You'll find it's handy for muddy sporting equipment and yard tools as well.

USE HARDY FLOORING Mudrooms work best when you have an easy-cleaning floor that shrugs off water and grime. Tile works best. Some laminates are good for mudrooms, Smock says, but make sure you have the kind that stands up to moisture well.

CONTAIN THOSE SHOES Park by the door some kind of

device for containing drippy shoes and boots the moment they enter the house. A shallow plastic "boot tray," available at hardware stores, can accommodate several pairs of shoes, Smock says. Or stack a set of plastic buckets by the door—one for each child in the family. When a child enters with slush-covered boots, drop the boots into a bucket to dry off.

BE READY TO WIPE Keep a container of disposable wipes by the door to mop up messy hands, shoes and doggy paws. If your family tracks in a lot of slushy grime, a couple of old towels will be a god-send. A stack of old news-papers will come in handy, too. If your shoes are soaked through, ball up sheets of newsprint and shove them inside the shoes. Change them every 20 minutes until they've sucked up all of the moisture.

GET ORGANIZED Mudrooms inevitably turn into "a little bit of a dumping ground" as people come a go, Smock says. So add some features that will keep personal items tidy and organized. Plenty of coat hooks are a must, and a locker, closet, or cubby storage is helpful, too. Supply a bench for sitting on while people take off shoes (the lidded kind of bench can double as storage for out-of-season items). Establish a spot for posting messages for family members. Set up a family "in box" (for mail, fliers, and such) and an "out box" (for that package that's headed for the post office and the library books that need to be returned). Key hooks will help everyone keep track of keys for the cars, bicycle locks, and shed.

SLEIGHT OF HAND

ONE MORE CLEANING DUTY TABLED

Dorothy Burling, a retiree in Misha-waka, Indiana, didn't like the way the outer rim of her circular patio table collected dirt. So she bought a stretch of cloth-backed Naugahyde® to use as a handsome cover to keep the dirt at bay. She cut the material 5 inches wider than the table itself, and she also cut a 4-inch hole in the center to accommodate the umbrella pole, which keeps the improvised cover in place when the wind blows. When the cover gets dirty, she tosses it into the washing machine.

YOUR OUTDOOR GEAR	Any possessions that spend a lot of time outdoors have to be rugged in the extreme. Grime, water, temperature extremes, and ultraviolet light all dam-

age their surfaces. Fortunately, this rugged nature makes them a breeze to clean and care for. Take the following easy steps to make your garden tools, grill, and patio furniture look better and last longer.

GET A HANDLE ON YOUR TOOLS

Caring for your garden tools is less about appearances and more about making them last. Start by investing a little more money for sturdier tools every time you need a new one. If you do, they'll be less likely to corrode and you won't have to spend time and money replacing them in the near future. Then, keeping your tools clean is simple, says garden expert Lance Walheim. Here's the bare minimum cleaning routine: At the end of your work session, lay your garden tools out on the ground. Use a putty knife to scrape off any caked-on dirt. Hose the tools off, wipe them dry, and store them out of the weather (in a shed, for instance). A quick hose-and-wipe will keep your outdoor power tools looking sharp as well, since most of them are now made watertight, says Dr. Trey Rogers, professor of turf grass management at Michigan State University in East Lansing, Michigan.

Are you willing to go a step further to clean and protect your garden tools? A thin coating of oil on your shovels, hoes, and trowels will prevent rust and make dirt less likely to cling to them. Try this old gardener's trick for giving your tools a super-quick oiling, says Walheim: Keep a bucket of oily sand in your shed. (You can just dump your used lawn mower oil in there, for instance, or add machine oil.) Whenever you have used one of your garden-ing tools, stab it into the sand for an instant coating, then hang it up. An alternative: Pour a little machine oil onto a rag and keep it handy for wiping off your tools. Wipe linseed oil onto the wooden handles of your tools to keep them from drying out, shrinking, and getting loose.

Sheds, of course, are all about protecting and storing tools in an orderly way. So don't hold back, says Walheim—cover every square inch of wall in your shed with pegboard and shelving. "That sure simplifies things," he says.

FOR THE GRILL OF YOUR DREAMS

The first priority for cleaning a barbecue grill is to get the grate grime-free because that's the part that comes into direct contact with your food. Either of these two approaches will save you a lot of scrubbing:

1. Remove the grate from the grill and drop it into a large plastic bag. Squirt it down with oven cleaner, close the bag with a twist-tie, and leave it for at least 2 hours. Then put on rubber gloves, remove the grate, wipe it down with a scrubber sponge, and hose it off.

2. If you have a self-cleaning oven, slide the grill grate(s) into the oven and run the appliance through its cleaning cycle.

To prevent food particles from clinging to the grates while you're cooking, spritz them with nonstick cooking spray before they get hot. When you're done cooking, scrape the grates with your metal spatula or a wire brush, then close the grill cover and let the grates cook in there for an extra 15 minutes. This will burn off excess food.

If you have a charcoal-burning grill, the only other crucial cleaning duty is getting rid of the ashes once the fire is totally out. Spread out a few sheets of newsprint on the lawn and dump the ashes onto it. Roll the paper up, folding the sides in to contain the ash, then drop the bundle into a plastic grocery bag and tie it off. Discard into an outdoor trash can.

THE GREAT OUTDOORS

REFURBISHING THE FURNITURE

Patio chairs, recliners, and tables seem like magnets for atmospheric grime. Suddenly their smooth and shiny surfaces are gray tinged and gritty. The solution: Give them a quick once-over with a high-pressure sprayer, says Tom Gustin of Merry Maids. To protect the finish of your patio furniture, use low pressure—1,200 to 1,350 psi. A general-purpose cleaner should be fine—unless it contains chlorine bleach, which will make the color of your furniture fade (particularly darker colors, such as brown and red).

To clean your patio umbrella, you may be able to get away with nothing more than a squirt from the garden hose. If stubborn grime is clinging to it, pour 1 gallon of warm water into a bucket and add a squirt of dishwashing liquid. Dip a brush (synthetic bristles) into the solution and scrub the umbrella. Then rinse with the hose.

If you have wooden furniture in your yard—or wooden fencing, for that matter—follow the same procedures for cleaning and sealing wooden decks.

Now that you have savored every word of this chapter, you are a certified Master of the Wild. Nothing that nature has to deliver can get past your pressure washer, squeegee, and mudroom. Okay, no one's going to fit you with a coonskin cap yet, and you won't be wrestling grizzlies anytime soon—but if one leaves a mess on your deck, you've got the situation under control!

CARS:
BACKSEAT ARCHAEOLOGY

I have donated my body to science. Not my flesh-and-blood body, mind you—my car's body. Far too much time, energy, money, and anxiety go into cleaning automobiles. The high-tech materials used to build our cars—both exteriors and interiors—are getting more durable every year. Shouldn't the effort expended in cleaning our cars diminish proportionately?

Here's how selflessly devoted I am to scientific inquiry: My car is 8 years old at this writing, and I haven't waxed it in 5. I don't wash it more than a few times a year either, not counting the occasional rinse if the buildup of road slush gets out of hand in the winter. I'm in good company. More than half of all Americans wash their cars less than once a month, and about 15 percent of American car owners never wash their cars at all.

My car looks . . . well, if not pristine it definitely looks okay. I'm betting the finish will still be in reasonable shape by the time the car is ready for the scrap heap. If my ride were some

ROADMAP
FOR CLEANLINESS

You're not going to make your car-buying decision based solely on how easy it is to clean the vehicle. Nevertheless, here are some points to keep in mind. After all, the more often you make easy-care choices, the saner your life will get.

- Black cars show dirt most readily. White cars look terrible in the winter when they've been splattered with slush. Of all car colors, silver stands up best to dirt and slush, and the color has a good resale record as well.

- SUVs take twice as long to clean as compacts, and it's really hard to reach certain parts of an SUV with a wash mitt—the center of the roof, for instance.

- Fabric upholstery is much easier to clean than leather.

- If the car dealer offers to treat your upholstery with fabric protectant to ward off spills and stains, save yourself the $80. The new upholstery materials are so advanced that it's probably not necessary. If you want extra protection anyway, buy a can of Scotchgard and spray it yourself.

kind of show car—say, a Lamborghini® or a Rolls-Royce®—boy, I would be out in the driveway every weekend washing and waxing with the best of them. Driving myself nuts. But no, my rig is a modest, lozenge-shaped compact like a zillion others you'll see on the road. It's a tool. It gets me from point A to point Z with reasonable fuel economy.

We see this advice printed with astounding frequency: "Protect your investment by washing and waxing your car regularly." Huh? How did we come to view cars as an investment? No matter how well you care for it, a car loses roughly 50 percent of its value every 4 years. So that $20,000 beauty you bought will be worth $10,000 after 4 years, $5,000 after 8 years and $2,500 after 12 years. If your 401-K performed like that you'd cover your investment adviser in honey and stake him or her to an anthill.

Here's a much more sane way to think about your car: To get the most value out of your car, drive it until the wheels fall off. Then sell it to a teenager for $215, use it as a trade-in on your next car, or donate it to charity and take the tax write-off. Remember, neither that teenager, the dealership, nor the charity will give a beep if the car isn't glimmering with a showroom finish.

The "you-gotta-wax-your-car-or-it-will-rust" sentiment is antiquated thinking—just begging us to cheat. In truth, carmakers in recent years have made enormous leaps in preventing corrosion, particularly in the use of galvanized sheet metal and high-tech clear coat finishes. Two decades ago, it was fairly common to spot the occasional rusted-out rattletrap creaking down the street. The way today's cars are built, that's a rare sight indeed.

The typical car finish is 100 microns thick, about the width of two human hairs, says Robert R. Matheson, Ph.D., an auto finish expert for DuPont®. There are four layers in this coating:

* Electrocoat, which prevents corrosion.
* Primer, which smooths out the surface and protects the electrocoat from UV rays.
* Base coat, which provides your car's color.
* And clear coat, the tough transparent shell that protects the finish from everyday wear.

The most exciting advancements are being made in clear-coat technology. Around the year 2001, says Matheson, clear coats got tough enough that you could finally run your vehicle through a commercial car wash without worry that the process would do more harm than good. The problem was that the automated brushes would rub surface grit into the car's finish, causing minuscule scratches. Those days are gone, which is good news for people who love to "outsource" their cleaning chores. And even better news: Waxing is unnecessary, too. On top of modern clear coats, wax offers such a slim extra whiff of protection that it's not worth the effort.

So, just who is proclaiming that you need to wash your car weekly and wax it once a month or so? Not surprisingly, it's car-wash operators and the people selling car-wash products.

Am I advocating that you stop washing your car, period? Not at all. There are some very good reasons to wash your car now and then:

* If your car is covered in slushy road salt or acidic, splattered bugs, which really can eat away at your car.

* If you live in a region affected by acid rain. This includes industrialized areas such as the northeastern United States, but it's even more of a problem in the South, where acid rain is aggravated by heat and humidity. In fact, the problem is so extreme in Jacksonville, Florida, that, according to Matheson, car-finish scientists test their products there.

* To slough off the gritty buildup on your car. Abrasion from road grit can work on your car's finish like sandpaper.

* If you just plain feel better when your car sparkles like a Las Vegas casino sign. That's perfectly valid. Do what makes you feel good.

Since there are valid reasons to wash your car, the crucial question becomes: How often? The party line is every 2 weeks or so—what car industry folks call "reasonable care." At that rate of washing, even the finish on the cheapest cars will look good for 6 or 7 years, and the more expensive rides will still be sharp after 10 or 12 years. Those life expectancies are right in line with the rust-through warranties that carmakers are now offering—6 years is common, and some models offer a

12-year guarantee. New-car buyers hold onto their cars an average of 7 years, which means that many folks are trading in their cars before the body is even out of warranty.

What's the worst that could happen if you never washed your car? Let's say you buy one of the most inexpensive new cars—which generally means you'll get a weaker finish—and you expose it to the worst conditions the environment has to offer. It *could* have a corrosion problem in as little as 4 years, says Matheson. That's not really a goal to aspire to. With just a little regular effort—say, washing every month or two, depending on conditions, and cleaning off those bugs and salt immediately—you'll add several years of life to that finish. Fortunately, there are plenty of easy, time-saving ways to get the job done. So before you strip down to your Speedo® and haul out the buckets and wash mitts, read on.

A LITTLE HELP FROM MOTHER NATURE

Here's how to perform the world's fastest car wash. Buy a car squeegee at an auto supply store and store it in your trunk. On a morning when there's a nice blanket of dew on everything outside, whip out your squeegee and wipe down the roof, windows, hood, trunk, and doors.

PAYING FOR CONVENIENCE

The pain-free way to wash your car, of course, is to pay someone else to do it—assuming you find someone who will do it right. Automatic car washes of old had huge twirling brushes that were capable of scratching circular swirls into the finish of your car. In a modern "conveyor" car wash—the type that moves your car along a track automatically—you're likely to find that a jungle of hanging, jiggling cloths does the cleaning. Or just a series of spray jets.

THE ROAD'S REVENGE

If your car gets splotched with tar or asphalt, clean it off right away, says Robert R. Matheson, Ph.D., an auto finish expert for DuPont. After 7 days to 10 days, tar and asphalt will bond with your car's paint and ruin the finish. Conventional car-washing detergent— combined with some elbow grease— will do the trick. (See the car-washing instructions in this chapter.) Or stop by an auto-supply store for a product designed specifically for removing such material.

Look for a car wash that advertises soft cloths or "no touch." Commercial car washes also have superior equipment and a staff that's more practiced at car washing than you are. So for the investment of a sawbuck and 10 minutes of your time, you'll probably come away happy. You'll get a clean exterior, clean windows, and a quick cleanup inside. (Detailing your car—a meticulous cleaning inside and out—can easily run you $100 or so.)

HANDING YOUR BABY OVER

Here's how to get the most out of an automatic car wash.

BUY IN QUANTITY Try out all the local car washes. When you find one you like—and if you've decided that outsourcing this job is the way to go—ask the cashier if they sell books of tickets at a discount. Some companies will even add the tip into the cost of the ticket. That way, you won't even have to open your wallet. You also can just hand a car-washing ticket to some other family member so he or she can get the job done for you.

GIVE THEM A RUNDOWN If there's anything peculiar about the way your car operates, be sure to tell the car wash attendant when you hand over your keys. Maybe your car is prone to locking itself automatically or it starts up in an unusual way. A few simple words in this case can save you a ton of grief.

WATCH THE WIPE DOWN At the end of the car wash process, you'll usually find a team of folks toweling off your vehicle. Stand nearby and pay attention to their work—this will inspire them to do a better job, particularly if you're holding a few dollar bills in your hand that may or may not become a tip. This is your time to speak up if you think anything's amiss with the cleaning job.

DON'T BE A STREAKER Once you've had your car washed, wait a couple of hours before you roll the windows down. There will be moisture trapped in the door, and rolling the window down will streak them with water—which will dry and leave spots. So give the water in the doors time to evaporate.

<table>
<tr><td>

TAKE THE
CASH OPTION

</td><td>

Want a little more control over how your car-washing is done? In a self-service car wash, you pull your car into a carport-like bay, feed money into the

</td></tr>
</table>

machine, and use a sprayer or brush to do the cleaning yourself. You can get in and out in 10 minutes or 15 minutes—quick enough that it still feels like cheating when compared to the elaborate production some folks mount on their driveways each weekend. In exchange for putting a little work into the operation, you're saving a few bucks compared to the cost of a full-service car wash. And you don't need to own any of the car-washing gear, other than towels to dry the car when you are done.

Here's how to get the best results from a self-service unit.

THINK AHEAD Before you head to the car wash, grab a couple of things around the house—including at least $5 in bills and quarters (you may not spend that much, but running out of cash when your car is still soapy really stinks). Also take along your drying towels. A couple of old, soft, 100 percent cotton towels will do. Alternatives are a natural chamois cloth or several of those smaller towels you can buy in auto-supply stores.

OVERPAY Most cash-operated car wash machines have a minimum fee just to get the water flowing, commonly $2. If you run out of time and your wash job isn't done, you'll have to pay

$2 more to get the washer going again. So overpay at the outset—two or three extra quarters ought to do it—to give yourself ample cleaning time.

GET IT WET Select the soap setting on the controls, and cover the car in soapy water from the high-pressure sprayer, working your way from top to bottom. Don't forget the wheels and wheel wells. Then set the sprayer on rinse, again working from top to bottom to get rid of all the soap. (If there's an applicator brush, make sure the car is wet before you touch the brush to the finish. Otherwise, you'll scratch the paint.)

NOW MOP UP Use the towels to dry your car. Drying is described more thoroughly in the car-washing instructions a little later, but basically it's best to dry in order of importance from a visual standpoint—windows first, then hood and trunk, followed by roof, sides, and wheels.

GO AND THEN STOP No matter how good a job you did toweling off your car, there still will be water hiding in the crevices. This water will dribble out once the car gets moving and will leave spots if left to dry on its own. So you're going to outwit the wet: Drive half a block and pull over. Mop up any drips that have appeared, and get on your way again.

PAY THE BALD GUY TO DO IT

Washing your car actually is an easy task. It's *drying* your car that takes most of the time and effort. So it's nice to hear of a product that allows you to eliminate the drying step altogether. At this writing, the Mr. Clean AutoDry Carwash® system is a unique product, but competitors are sure to follow. The initial kit will cost you around $20, which you might find worth it if you want to wash your chariot in the driveway regularly but like to keep the effort and time involved to a minimum.

The system comes with a spray handle, a replaceable water filter that slides into the handle, and a container of refill soap.

GETTING THE MOST FROM A COIN-OP CAR WASH

Whenever you're about to depart for a self-service, coin-operated car wash, a little alarm should go off in your head. Maybe there are other objects around the house that would benefit from a quick, high-pressure soap-and-rinse session as long as you're going to be camped out in the car wash bay anyway.

Make sure any possessions you clean this way can stand up to the high-pressure spray without falling to pieces. Good candidates include the charcoal grill, outdoor furniture, wagons, tricycles, wheelbarrows, garbage cans, shovels, and rakes. Pull them out onto the floor of the washing bay and hose them down quickly at the same time you're cleaning the car. (Make sure you paid for enough time to handle everything.) Bring an extra towel or two to wipe these items down before you load them back into the car.

Of course, to haul bulkier items you'll need a station wagon or van. Even better: Put everything in the bed of a pickup truck and wash them right there, hosing out the truck bed as a final step. No need to unload them from the truck at all.

Be considerate of the folks who own the car wash. Chunky debris could clog the drains, according an industry source. So dump all of the ashes out of your grill and remove the moldy newsprint from the bottom of that garbage can before you leave the house.

You connect the handle to your garden hose and wet your car down with regular water. Then you change the handle to the soap setting, squirt soap all over the car, wash with a car-washing mitt or sponge, and rinse again. Final step: Set the handle on the auto-dry setting and squirt the entire car again with the "deionized" water. This water has been treated so that it sheets off the car quickly and dries without leaving mineral spots.

Not a bad deal for fans of corner-cutting gizmos.

LAST RESORT: THE HANDS-ON APPROACH

If you've made it this far into the chapter, you must be yearning for an honest-to-goodness, hands-on car-washing session in your driveway. That's okay, I'll help you anyway—and there are still plenty of ways to cut corners.

You probably know people who turn driveway car-washing into a bigger production than *The Lion King*—a 4-hour extravaganza starring several helpers, enough water to fill five hot tubs, and a dozen bottles of exotic cleaning substances. Let's simplify that: With the following approach—much of it suggested by Philip Reed, senior consumer advice editor at the car information company Edmunds.com[SM]—you can clean the exterior of your car in 15 minutes flat all by yourself.

FIRST, GATHER THE GEAR

Drop by an auto-supply store and pick up a few items. These will help you do the job so quickly that you'll never dread it again—absolutely worth the investment:

* **A car-washing wand.** This device usually consists of a telescoping handle with a brush or pad on the end.

Some models hook up to your garden hose, and with others you pull on a plunger to suck soapy water from a bucket into the handle. As an alternative you could buy a wash mitt—a fuzzy glove that looks like part of a *Star Wars* Wookie costume—but you'll find that reaching some parts of the car will be harder with this approach.

❋ **A car squeegee.** This is an incredibly fast way to dry not only your car's windows but other flat surfaces as well—the hood and trunk, for instance. Make sure the blade is pliable.

❋ **A wheel brush.** These brushes are specially designed to remove grime from the complex crevices of automobile wheels. The bristles are 2 inches to 3 inches long, flexible and sturdy.

❋ **A container of tire black.** for an easy, glitzy final touch. Get the kind with a wipe-on applicator. If you use the spray-on kind, some of the tire black can get on the wheels and attract dirt.

The other items you'll need can probably be found around the house: two buckets, a garden hose, a bottle of car cleaner (make sure it's specifically made for cars—just about any other cleaner, such as dishwashing detergent, will be too harsh for a car's finish), and a natural chamois cloth or an old beach towel (you can buy terry towels specifically made for car washing, but since these things are barely bigger than a washcloth you'll need several to do the job).

NOW GET IT WET

Now consider where you're going to do the wash job. Direct sunlight won't do. The water you use will dry on the car's surfaces too quickly, leaving spotty deposits. Also, cold water splashed onto a hot car can cause spidery little cracks in the finish called crazing. So find a shady spot, preferably not under a tree that will drip sap or one that's holding a bird convention. Also, find a place where the wash water will flow off and disperse into the soil. Letting wash chemicals pour into a storm drain isn't a good idea.

Gear gathered, location chosen and hose hooked up, you're ready for the world's quickest at-home, bumper-to-bumper wash job. Follow these easy steps—in order.

1. Hose the car down. Get every inch of the surface wet. You want as much of the grime to loosen and flow away as possible. Any time you're squirting water at your car, try to keep it flowing in the direction it would go if you were driving through a rainstorm. Otherwise, you might force a quart or two of water into a vent or crevice where you don't want it to go.

2. Pour a gallon of water (cold is generally fine—check the directions on your cleaner) into one of the buckets and add the car cleaner according to the package directions— probably just an ounce or so if you're using a concentrate. Fill the second bucket with clean water for rinsing your brush. With the hose turned off, telescope your car-washing wand out to full length and use it to apply the soapy water. Don't scrub—let a light swish of the soapy brush loosen the dirt. Leave the wheels alone for the moment.

Aside from that, cover all outer surfaces of the car, including the windows and wheel wells. Dunk the brush into the rinse bucket frequently—so you're not dragging any accumulated grit across the car's finish—and then dip it into the cleaning solution again to continue soaping the car. If your brush touches the ground at all, rinse it before you touch it to the car again.

3. Rinse the car. If you have the type of washing wand that hooks up to a hose, rinse the brush one more time, turn the water on, and rinse the car, working top to bottom. If your wand isn't connected to a hose, use the spray nozzle on your hose to rinse the car. Again, leave the wheels alone for the moment.

4. Now you're in a race to dry the car before it dries on its own, leaving spots. If you're using a chamois cloth, wet it with the hose (not in that grubby bucket of rinse water) and squeeze it out. The chamois is now ready for super-absorption. But do *not* dry the car top to bottom, as you might be tempted to do. Dry the parts of the car in order

SLUSH BUSTER

If it's winter and little stalactites of gray, salty grime are hanging from the underside of your car, you can wash it all off in just seconds and forestall future corrosion. Go to your shed and grab the lawn sprinkler (you remember—the twirly little summer item?). Hook it up to the hose, turn the water on and, using the hose as a guiding pole, slide it under your car. Reposition it every 15 seconds until the entire bottom has been spritzed.

of importance. The windows come first. Nothing screams "clean car" like sparkling glass. Also, the cleaner the windows, the better the driver's visibility. Squeegee the windows quickly, wiping up any excess water at the corners and edges with your drying cloth. Then use your squeegee and cloth to dry the next-most-visible parts of the car: the hood and trunk. Towel off the roof, then dry the sides of the car. Use a light touch with any drying rag—a blotting action is best, rather than wiping. Pressing down on the rag as you wipe could harm the finish.

FINAL TOUCHES

Wheels and tires are the crowning glory of a car-wash job—where the rubber meets the road, as they say. The wheel covers are a particular challenge, as they can get covered in brake dust and many covers have a stylish design with hard-to-clean nooks and crannies. (Can you say "fashion victim"?) Dip the wheel brush into the bucket of car-cleaning solution and give each wheel and tire a 15-second scrub. Rinse with fresh water and dry with the cloth. Then apply the tire black to the rubber (following the package directions) for a glossy, fresh-off-the-showroom-floor finish.

Occasionally your car will pick up a stubborn blotch that defies conventional washing—hardened bug bodies or sap, for instance. Don't scrub at these—you'll do more harm than good. Go to your auto-supply store and buy one of the myriad products designed just for your problem. They generally require you to clean the car first, so now's the time to deal with it.

Also, if you insist on waxing your car, do it now. Reed says he never waxes his own car, and he doesn't know anyone who does. If you're going to wax, at least cheat a little bit: Pick one of the liquid waxes and follow the package directions. They're easier to apply than the firmer paste that comes in a tub.

CLEAR SAVINGS WITH
EASY GLASS CLEANER

For pennies, you can make enough glass cleaner to drown a hippopotamus. With the following approach, you not only save gobs of money, you simplify your life, too. Just mix up the windshield washer fluid in a jug and pour it into the little tank under your car's hood as needed. When you need glass cleaner for your home's windows, just dilute this homemade washer fluid with water. You'll never have to buy any kind of glass cleaner again!

- **TO MAKE WINDSHIELD WASHER FLUID.** Rinse out a gallon milk jug. Pour in 3 cups of rubbing alcohol and 10 cups of water. Add a squirt of dishwashing liquid. You can add one drop of blue food coloring so your solution looks like the commercial stuff—this also will remind people that the contents are not just water. Seal the jug. With a permanent marker, label the jug "Windshield Washer Fluid / Glass Cleaner Concentrate." Rubbing alcohol is toxic, so keep your jug away from children and idiotic adults. Store it, for instance,

on a high shelf in the garage. The rubbing alcohol will prevent freezing.

- **TO MAKE GLASS CLEANER.** When your squirt bottle of commercial glass cleaner runs out, save it. Go to your garage, where you'll find—if you've been paying attention—a jug labeled "Windshield Washer Fluid / Glass Cleaner Concentrate." Fill your squirt bottle one third of the way with this fluid and fill it the rest of the way with water. You can do the same mixing job, of course, in one of those empty squirt bottles you can buy at the supermarket, discount stores, or home supply stores. Label the squirt bottle "Glass Cleaner" in permanent marker.

If you need a larger quantity of glass cleaner—say, for cleaning the outside of your home's windows with a sponge-and-squeegee wand—prepare the amount you need in a bucket using the same proportions: one part homemade concentrate to two parts water.

A BREATH OF FRESH AIR

You can let the candy wrappers and doughnut bags pile up as high as you please on the floor of your car—your wheels will still get you to the supermarket and back without a complaint. But if you're ignoring a basic cleaning issue right there under your hood—the air filter—you're slowly choking your car to death.

The conventional wisdom is that you have to change your air filter every 10,000 miles or so. The hands-down easiest way to deal with a dirty air filter is to have your mechanic swap it out the next time you take your wheels in for an oil change. But if you can tell a hammer from a screwdriver and like to do your own light maintenance on your car, changing the air filter is simple task. And if you've been changing your own air filter every 10,000 miles, you'll want to know about the innovative K&N® Filter. This baby is good for 50,000 miles. And if you follow the manufacturer's simple directions for brushing, spraying, and rinsing the filter, it will be good for another 50,000. That saves you a whole lotta hood-popping, hand-griming work.

While the conventional replacement air filter is made of paper, the K&N Filter draws air through oil-covered cotton to snag impurities and to allow top-notch airflow at the same time, according to the car info experts at Edmunds.com. You won't be surprised to learn that it costs several times more than a conventional air filter, but if you like to reduce work and hassle, this is clearly the way to go. You can pick one up at your local auto parts store. The warranty on the filter is good for 10 years or, for goodness sake, 1 million miles.

If this inspires you to pop the hood on your car for the first time in a long while, the air filter lies inside that large, black plastic casing that's typically hovering right over the engine (sometimes to the side). Let the engine cool first. In most models, you can just pop open the clasps on the side of the casing with a screwdriver (sometimes there are screws to remove). Lift the cover, and you'll find the filter inside. If it's showing a lot of dirt buildup, you know your filter is impeding airflow and reducing your engine's performance. Time for a change!

It's amazing how a few small changes will make you feel so much better about the interior of your car. If you only have 90 seconds to invest, try this:

* First, do a little backseat archaeology. Open a car door, grab the first fast-food bag you can find, cram all of the other miscellaneous trash into it, and throw it away. You'll do this more frequently, by the way, if you have a trash can stationed near the driveway—in a handy corner of the garage, for instance.

* Pull out the floor mats, give them a shake, and put them back in.

* If you have crystal-clean windows, passengers will forgive the other foibles inside your car. So squirt glass cleaner onto a couple of paper towels and wipe down all the windows. Don't use glass cleaner on the plastic windows of a convertible, however. Hose them off with water and blot them dry with a towel. (Don't scrub or wipe in circles—that could scratch them.) Then apply a clear-plastic cleaner according to the package directions (spray-and-wipe products are available at auto stores).

HAND VAC: WINDS OF CHANGE

Maybe you're on a roll now, and you're ready to go for the full *How to Cheat at Cleaning* all-out supreme deluxe 5-minute interior detailing. If so—if you really want to commit to the next tier of car interior cleanliness—then invest in a battery-powered hand vacuum. Why? Because of the Accessibility Theorem: "A cleaning task will be accomplished on a frequency that is

TAMING THE TRUNK JUNK

Does the inside of your car trunk look like a junkyard on wheels? Here's a simple way to keep the contents of your car's trunk under control: Store some kind of container back there where you can stuff all the miscellaneous items—tools, flashlight, work gloves, jumper cables, medical kit, maps, and such.

The size of the container should leave plenty of room for the things you commonly haul temporarily (tennis racquets, book bags, and grocery sacks, for instance). The container also should have handles so you can lift it out to make room for the occasional enormous item you need to jam in there. You'll also be glad that everything's contained if you have to retrieve your spare tire from underneath the trunk floor. One quick lift and all your paraphernalia is out of the way.

My favorite trunk container: A plastic "milk crate" from a discount store. It's cheap, lightweight, has handles, and you can see through the sides to find what you're looking for. If you're hankering to throw more money at this matter, an auto supply store will happily sell you a car trunk organizer with multiple storage bins and pockets. However, an old gym bag would serve just as well as the one I inspected.

inversely proportional to the distance between the object to be cleaned and the materials necessary to clean it." That is, if it's a hassle to get to your cleaning gear, no cleaning gets done.

Now, in the case of an automobile interior, vacuuming is a core function. But dragging the home vacuum cleaner out to the driveway is a chore for anybody. Then you have to hunt around for a really long extension cord. For a lot of people the situation is worse: They have to clean their cars on the street or in an alleyway, well out of reach of the home Hoover. So a battery-powered hand vac, or one that connects to your cigarette lighter, is the solution: Just store it in the trunk, and you'll never again moan about cleaning the inside of your auto. (Don't store it in the backseat—some kid will decide to vacuum the back of your head while you're changing lanes on the freeway.) If you have the kind of hand vacuum with a wall-mounted recharging station, you might want to hang it in the garage, where it will be close by.

Whatever kind of vacuum you're using, here's how to clean the interior in 5 minutes or less:

1. As above, pull out all of the trash—anything too big for the vacuum—and throw it away.

2. Pull out the mats, shake them, vacuum them, and then vacuum the interior carpet. Move the front seats forward and back to get to some of the hidden—and often grungy—parts of the carpet. If your vacuum has a narrow nozzle, use it to get beside and between the seats and to vacuum any other nooks and crannies you can find.

3. Use an upholstery attachment to vacuum the seats. If you use seat covers or seat pads pull them out, give them a shake to remove the debris they've collected, and then pop them back into place. (Auto-supply stores sell car seat covers that will protect your original seats from damage—or hide the rips and stains you already have. There are two basic approaches: fabric that closely covers the entire seat, or L-shaped pads that cushion your back and your buns. These are particularly handy if kids, dogs, or fraternity brothers frequent your automobile.)

SLEIGHT OF HAND

LEAD THEM BY THE NOSE

Can scented products really re-create "that new car smell" for your automobile? Forget it, says Philip Reed, senior consumer advice editor at the car information company Edmunds.com. "New car smell cannot—I repeat, cannot—be duplicated. Many have tried. No one has succeeded," he says.

Still, there's something to be said for a pleasant-smelling car. The passengers in your jalopy will overlook a dusty instrument panel if your interior smells fresh. You can create this illusion at no cost from readily available materials in your home. Just toss an unused dryer sheet under one of the front car seats. The sunny odor will quickly permeate the interior. Alternatively, pour 4 ounces of ground coffee into an old sock, wire it closed with a twisty-tie, and put that under your car seat. Or do the same thing with scented cat litter.

4. Assuming you just washed the outside of your car, take your still-wet chamois, sit in the driver's seat, and look around. Wipe up any dust and dirt that's within your sight. (After all, you're the one who spends the most time in this car, so your viewpoint rules.) Wipe the dashboard, the area around the instruments, the glass over the instruments, the steering wheel, the horn area and the steering column. Wipe the cup holders, the center console and cubby. Keep changing to a fresh part of the chamois as you go.

NOW STOW YOUR STUFF

You're done! Time to gather up all your implements and put them away. Keep the hand vacuum in the trunk or hanging in the garage so you can use it whenever the whim strikes. Try to keep all of the other gear—the washing wand, chamois, car cleaner and such—together in one place. You could stash everything in a bucket, for instance, and park the bucket near the garden hose for easy access next time you need to clean your car. Assuming you ever feel the need again.

BABIES, TODDLERS, AND PETS: THE THINGS WE DO FOR LOVE

We invite little creatures into our homes—both the human kind and the animal kind—and what do we get in return? A relentless source of pee and poop. Not to mention hand and paw prints everywhere, floors littered with toys, food flung about wantonly, and furniture and clothing festooned with animal fur.

Making it all worth it, however, are mountains of love, devotion, and companionship. Not for a moment will I suggest you forego parenthood or pet ownership. 'Tis better to have loved and lived in filth than to have never loved at all. But you can actually *have* it all—the kids, the pets, an orderly home, and even your sanity—as long as you keep a few core concepts in mind:

* Be willing to spend money in exchange for convenience (one of the primary rules from Chapter 1).
* A little training pays off big-time for both children and pets.
* The less exposure you have to excrement, the happier you'll be.

The first 6 months of parenthood is a hazy, sleep-deprived confusion punctuated by periods of unbridled joy and horrifying surprises. Complicating matters further, when you're new to parenting a torrent of possessions flood into your home that you have never had to manage before—diapers, baby blankets, bottles, ointments, baby clothes, mobiles, teensy food jars, a high chair, a baby swing, a stroller, and thousands of stuffed animals. If there ever was a time for convenience items, organizing tricks, corner cutting, and cleaning cheats, this is it.

Most of the baby-related items that clutter a new parent's home can be easily organized by "stations"—just like the adult stations described in Chapter 3 for food preparation, mailing, crafts, and more. So you want an assigned spot for each diaper-changing item within easy reach of the changing table, an assigned spot for each sleep-related item near the crib, and an assigned spot for each bath-related item near the tub. Plotting out where every little baby thing goes may sound terribly persnickety, but the failure to make these decisions is the road to ruin, says Dana Korey, a professional organizer based in Del Mar, California.

"I think people really need to decide what they need in each space—make the decision to decide," she says. "The better you contain your items and divide them up by category, the easier it will be to maintain your system."

The diaper-changing station is a prime example, she says. Think about it: When your baby is on the changing table, you want to be able to keep one hand on her so she doesn't roll off. This means that all paraphernalia related to changing should be within super-easy grabbing distance—preferably on a nearby shelf in lidless bins so that you don't have to struggle to open things with your one free hand. Having to open a cabinet or a closed container will get old by your 2,000th diaper change. Position everything in the order you typically use them for a diaper change—for instance, wipes first, then ointment, then powder, and then fresh diapers. Make sure there's a pedal-operated diaper pail at your feet.

DIAPERS: CHANGE IS GOOD

Speaking of diapers, few things will have as big an effect on a new parent's sanity as the kind of diapers you choose. When you have your first child, you may develop this vague notion that using cloth diapers, rather than disposable ones, is somehow more wholesome, more pure, more environmentally friendly, and more healthful for the baby. Because nothing is too good for your offspring—who will, after all, win a Nobel Prize some day—you're going to smugly turn your nose up at disposable diapers and wrap your child's bottom in cushy cotton. After a couple months of leaky diapers, diaper changes every other minute, and shocking messes to launder, you'll realize your monumental mistake—a classic "What was I thinking?" situation.

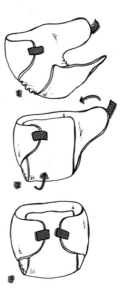

The experts who analyze such things scientifically say that the pure-and-natural reputation of cloth diapers is a huge misconception. The truth is that in terms of health, cost, and environmental impact, neither cloth diapers nor disposable diapers are superior—it's a wash, so to speak. But in terms of convenience, disposables are unquestionably the winner. So leap,

A BOXFUL OF MEMORIES

Crayon scrawls, finger paintings, Popsicle® stick sculptures—the urge to save these treasures is irresistible. However, your child's creative work can quickly inundate the shelves and counters in your home. Also, works you hope to preserve will quickly become tattered when they're lying in random heaps. Professional organizer C. Lee Cawley, of Arlington, Virginia, has the solution: Set up memorabilia boxes for each child.

A wide, flat storage box will do the trick. Cawley likes 14½-inch by 11½-inch cardboard boxes. They're 3 inches deep and have metal corners, plus slots on the side for labels. To help preserve the contents without paying the high price of official archival boxes, line each box with two layers of acid-free archival tissue paper, which you can buy at storage or craft stores, or online.

Label each box with the child's name and grade range—for instance, "Christina, Preschool–1." When your child brings artwork home, pick out the best piece of the week and put it in her box. Don't mix papers you're saving for posterity with papers that are important here and now—the T-ball schedule, for instance. The memorabilia boxes will be powerful keepsakes to give to your children when they reach middle age.

wholeheartedly and guilt-free, into the convenience of disposables.

Managing disposable diapers is easy, but from a cleanliness standpoint there are some things to remember. The one drawback to disposables is that they contain the poop and pee so well that it can be hard to tell when it's time to change them. At least once an hour, stick a finger into the waistband of your baby's diaper and look in to see if anything inter-esting is going on. Wearing a loaded diaper for too long will give a baby diaper rash.

If you have solid poop in a diaper, shake it out into the toilet and flush before you throw the diaper out. Roll the used diaper up into a ball and use the waistband tapes to secure it before you toss it into a plastic-lined diaper pail (remember, you want a pedal-operated lid). This way, the diaper will take up less space and will contain its own filth and odor somewhat. Wash your hands immediately after each diaper change. Once a day, take the diapers out to the garbage can and replace the diaper pail liner. (You can do it less often if you pick up those special odor-reducing trash can liners at the supermarket.) Once a week, spritz the pail with disinfecting cleaner inside and outside, and wipe with a paper towel.

So there—with that one diapering decision you're going to save yourself a ton of grief and grime. But there are plenty of other sanity-preserving strategies that parents can implement. Let's take a look.

TIME FOR CLEANING TRIAGE

New parents know the word *overwhelmed* intimately. Jen Singer, a writer on parenting and a stay-at-home mom, says that when a baby arrives it's time to revise your standards for home cleaning. Stick to a few narrowly defined priorities, tasks that directly affect your life—"cleaning triage," she calls this. For instance:

* You have to have a steady supply of onesies for the baby to wear, so get the laundry done.
* Empty the diaper and garbage pails daily to keep stink and messes under control.
* Ignore the dishes until the end of the day, when the kids are in bed.
* Let the dusting go, unless your mother-in-law is coming over.
* Vacuum the floors once a week.
* Clean the main bathroom, but leave the others alone.
* Let everything else go.

Singer has two rarely used rooms in her house. To limit cleaning chores, she shuts the doors to those rooms and leaves them alone until they're needed—for holidays, for instance. "I can shut the doors to the living room and leave it for a month," she says.

THE INCREDIBLE VANISHING JUNK HEAP

Children are not renowned for keeping their bedrooms neat. You can start training your kids to keep an orderly environment at the toddler stage, however. (You can reasonably expect them to perfect these skills by the time they're, say, in their early 30s.) Here's the secret for instantly creating the appearance of order in a household with children, particularly if you have visitors: Close the doors to their bedrooms.

It's a tad trickier to keep the rest of the house neat and clean when the kids play outside of their bedrooms, but the following corner-cutting ideas will help you there as well. (Make sure you also check out Chapter 4 for advice on getting kids to help with household cleaning.)

PUT PLAYTHINGS IN THEIR PLACE

Toddler toys are a lot like liquids—that is, they spread out to cover any space that contains them. To preserve your sanity, Singer recommends a few simple toy-management measures:

* Institute no-toy zones in the house. No toys may enter the home office, for instance. If possible, confine all toys to one playroom—or even the child's bedroom.

* Supply a generous number of toy boxes. At specific times of the day, have the kids participate in putting toys away. In this situation, brainwashing your kids is perfectly acceptable, so sing the Barney® cleanup song.

* Limit the influx of toys. If Grandpa hauls a new toy into the house every time he visits, establish some ground rules. Tell him, "You know, you've become Santa Claus to these kids—every time you arrive, they expect a toy. I'd rather they appreciate you for you."

- Encourage the outflow of toys. Before any birthday or gift-giving holiday, go through all the toys with your kids and decide which ones can be thrown out or donated to charity. Take your children on the ride with you to the Salvation Army℠, so they learn a lesson about giving to people in need. "I call this 'making room for Santa,'" Singer says. "Santa won't come unless you get rid of some of this stuff."

GET A VIDEO BOX FOR THE TOTS If you have a small child in the house, store all of his videos in one lidless box that he can easily reach on a low shelf, says professional organizer C. Lee Cawley, of Arlington, Virginia. The typical humongous living room entertainment center—the kind with myriad doors and drawers—is too complex for a little kid to work with. The result: The child never learns to find his own video, watch it, and return it to its storage area. The parents get to do all of the work. An open box stuffed with Thomas the Tank Engine® videos may not be the trendiest decorating scheme, but at least your child can clean up after himself and keep clutter under control.

GET THE HANG OF COAT RACKS Coat racks are a kid-friendly accessory, says Alexandria Lighty, owner of the House Doctors Handy Man Service℠ in New York City. If you have one in the foyer, your children will readily use the coat rack rather than tossing their jackets onto the floor when they enter the house. Stationed in a child's bedroom, a coat rack is a handy place to hang pajamas or any other clothing that has trouble finding its way to the closet. These clothes may be more visible than if they were in the closet, but at least they're up off the floor.

BUY AN AMPLE NIGHT STAND Many parents make the mistake of purchasing a cute little night stand to go beside a toddler's bed—one that's barely big enough to hold a little lamp, says Korey. Get one that's large enough to accommodate all the things a youngster might need while in bed, including the lamp, a book, a water glass, tissues, and a flashlight.

An organizer that hangs off the side of a child's bed also makes a handy spot to stash items that a youngster might want in the middle of the night, Korey says. Such organizers typically have a "tongue" that slides between the mattress and the box spring, allowing several shoe-bag-style storage pockets to dangle down the side of the bed. What's more, it creates a solution to clutter without eating up shelf or dresser-top space.

THE FEEDING FRENZY

We've already discussed how to manage what comes *out* of your baby—the end product, so to speak. But putting food *into* your baby makes almost as much of a mess. Here's how to cope.

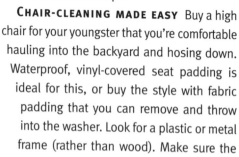

CHAIR-CLEANING MADE EASY Buy a high chair for your youngster that you're comfortable hauling into the backyard and hosing down. Waterproof, vinyl-covered seat padding is ideal for this, or buy the style with fabric padding that you can remove and throw into the washer. Look for a plastic or metal frame (rather than wood). Make sure the high chair has a removable plastic tray that you can wash in the sink or just plop into the dishwasher. The tray on the highchair should have a high rim, which will keep some percentage of the baby's food off of the floor.

WHEN THE FOOD FLIES ... Don't even consider feeding your baby unless you have a couple of basic accessories on hand, says Judi Sturgeon, a professional house cleaner and home health aid based in Ambler, Pennsylvania:

 * A baby bib with a pocket at the bottom for catching food (this will keep the pureed peas off the furniture and floor). When the bib isn't in use or being laundered, give it a permanent spot hanging off the back of the high chair.
 * A clean, damp cloth for easy wiping of face, hands, and surfaces, so the mashed carrots don't get smeared all over the house.

DESIGN DIRT AWAY

TAKE THE TOOLBOX TO TIMMY'S ROOM

If your child's bedroom was originally outfitted for adult use, make some minor hardware adjustments that will allow him to clean up after himself, says Alexandria Lighty, owner of the House Doctors Handy Man Service in New York City. These adjustments include the following:

 * Hooks on the inside of the closet door, low enough that small kids can hang jackets on them.
 * Double hanging rods in the closet— one high and one low. This makes best use of space, and your child will be able to hang up and retrieve his own clothes from the lower rod.
 * Plenty of additional shelving, " because they have so many things they want to display," Lighty says.

Even kids who are 2 years or 3 years old can start taking ownership of the organization of their possessions— finding their toys in a simple bin, for instance, and putting them back when they're finished with them.

OUT OF THE HIGH CHAIR, INTO THE TUB Arrange your household schedule so that bath time comes right after dinnertime. This way, you don't have to do a perfect job of cleaning the baby's face and hands. The bath will take care of that.

HANDY HABITS Training your toddler to adopt these habits will save you tons of cleaning, says Sturgeon:

* Eating over the plate—a good lifelong habit that will keeps crumbs and dribbles contained.
* Washing her hands *after* eating, so she doesn't smudge the walls, floors, doors, and furniture.
* Washing hands as soon as she comes inside the house, so she doesn't bring dirt and germs home from day care or the backyard.

THE FURRY CLEANUP CREW Having a dog in the home at the same time that you have a baby is not a bad idea at all. I have a cousin who eliminated 90 percent her baby-spill cleanups by allowing her eager dog to lap food up off of the floor.

> ### YOUR FURRY FRIENDS

Two factors are crucial to mess-free pet ownership, says Melissa Laiserin, a PetSmart[SM] dog behavior expert based in Phoenix, Arizona:

* Training your pet to do what's appropriate.
* Supervising your pet to correct behavior and forestall disasters.

Naturally, the primary behaviors you're concerned about are peeing and pooping. The key to potty training is watching your pet closely for signs that he has to relieve himself. So, when you first bring your pet into the home, make sure you can spend plenty of time close to him. If your dog is walking in circles and sniffing, or running back and forth, he's gotta go—move him quickly to his official potty spot. This is usually either a spot in the yard outside, a puppy training pad inside, or a container of litter, which is available now for small dogs. If you find your dog squatting inside, you're too late.

Reward your dog when he gets it right. Depending on the dog, the reward might be a small treat, verbal praise, or a scratch behind the ear. (Although I'm using dogs as an example, Laiserin says that the same training rules apply to cats as well—it's a myth that they can't be trained.)

Learn your pet's "bathroom" schedule. A dog will typically need to relieve himself within 20 minutes of eating and drinking, within a half hour of vigorous exercise, and first thing in the morning. As a precaution, let him relieve himself just before you go to bed, too. Puppies can delay relieving themselves for 1 hour per month of age, Laiserin says. This means your 4-month-old woojums will need to go out at least every 4 hours.

Good training also will help prevent destructive behavior, Laiserin says. First, eliminate the temptations. Make sure there's a lid on your kitchen garbage can, for instance; and, if possible, position it behind closed doors. Dogs particularly love smelly socks, so put them in a hamper, not on the floor. Make sure the kids keep their toys picked up. And consider the messages you're sending the animal during playtime. If you play tug-of-war using a worn-out sneaker, can you blame your dog for chewing up a perfectly good one the next day?

Sprays are available in pet stores that will help train your animals to avoid certain places (your home office, for instance) and to quit chewing on certain objects (the couch cushions). Also, the folks who make invisible fences for the yard (the dog gets an annoying shock from his collar when he strays out of bounds) are now offering similar systems for interior use. This allows you to make rooms or entire floors of your house off-limits to animals.

Now let's take a look at easy ways for pet owners to cope when preventive measures fail.

PET ACCIDENTS: "IT" HAPPENS

As with so many other cleaning tasks, disposables are the very best cheat-at-cleaning approach when you're fixing pet messes. Particularly with feces or urine, you want products that eliminate the yuck factor—allowing you to have minimal exposure in terms of sight, touch, and odor. Disposable cat boxes that come prefilled with litter certainly fill the bill. You can find any number of ingenious poop-scooping devices that allow you to quickly slide pet feces straight into a plastic sack that you can drop right into a waste bin.

Now and then, however, you come face-to-face with the pet-owner's nightmare—pee or poop right on the dining room carpet. This is a serious situation. Not because it will tie your stomach in a knot, but because you can't afford to let the odors linger even subtly in your carpet. If your pet detects waste odors in the future,

PET BOWLS: HIDE THE EVIDENCE

A lot of people feed their pets on the kitchen floor, but you can use a more out-of-the-way place for feeding if you don't like the sight of the pet's bowls—and the food that gets flung about—in your kitchen. Find a place with a hard (preferably tile) floor for easy cleaning. You also want quick access to water for bowl refills and a nearby place to store the pet food. A utility room, laundry room, or mudroom would probably do nicely.

To keep messes under control, place your pet's food and water bowls on a tray or a plastic mat with a raised rim. Wash the mat and bowls weekly in hot water and dishwashing liquid, then rinse and dry.

she may think this spot has become her new official bathroom, and history will repeat itself.

Solid poop is the easiest to cope with. Fold three paper towels on top of each other and tent them over the poop. Lift the excrement straight up into the towels, then either drop it into a plastic bag and tie it off to throw away, or drop the poop (not the towels) into the toilet and flush. If there are traces left on the floor or carpet, mix a cup of warm water with a squirt of dishwashing liquid and blot at the spot until it's gone, then rinse with fresh water. Finally, fold up two paper towels until they're the size of the wet spot and press down firmly with your fist for a minute to draw up the water.

For anything messier—say, runny poop, pee, or vomit—you need a special weapon: an enzyme-based cleaner. No pet owner should be without this stuff—it's the one sure way to eliminate the lingering odors from pet accidents. Follow the directions on the package of your cleaner. The procedure will go something like this: First, dispose of any solids as described above. Then, use the blotting method with fresh paper towels to sop up most of the liquid. Apply the enzyme-based cleaner and leave it for the prescribed amount of time (it can take hours or even days for the enzymes to thoroughly break down the organic material that

FAST·FORMULAS

THE CURE
FOR FURRY FURNITURE

What makes pet hair cling so vehemently to your furniture and drapes? A static charge. Here's a little trick that will kill that electrical grip and make hair cleanup easy, says Lisa Peterson, the Newton, Connecticut–based spokesperson for the American Kennel Club[SM].

Fill a spray bottle one quarter of the way with liquid fabric softener and the rest of the way with water, seal the bottle, and shake. Stand near your hair-covered furniture or drapes and mist the air with the solution (don't squirt it directly onto the fabric). The hair will lose its static charge and fall to the floor. Now all you have to do is vacuum. You'll find that the nonclinging hair gets vacuumed up without the least bit of resistance.

An alternative: Warm up a drier sheet in the drier and wipe it across your furniture and drapes to kill the charge.

HAIR ON THE SIDE OF CAUTION

Are you reluctant to buy a dog, fearing that a pooch might leave a blanket of fur on the furniture and carpet? Do you get itchy eyes and a runny nose run when you're around dogs? Here's a list of dog breeds that are known for minimal shedding of hair and minimal shedding of the dander that annoys allergy sufferers, according to the American Kennel Club.

- Bedlington terrier
- Bichon frise
- Chinese crested (they're hairless!)
- Irish water spaniel
- Kerry blue terrier
- Maltese
- Poodles
- Portuguese water dog
- Schnauzer
- Soft-coated wheaten terrier
- Xoloitzcuintli (hairless)

would otherwise cause lingering odors). Then rinse again with water, blot with paper towels, and let it dry. Now, that wasn't so bad, was it?

THEY PUT THE "FUR" IN FURNITURE

Next to pee, poop, and vomit, pet hair on your clothing and furniture seems like a refreshing little diversion. But your own tolerance for furry clothing and furniture is bound to wear thin. You're going to want some easy ways to keep it off your furnishings and to clean it up if your prevention efforts fail.

People often associate allergies with pet hair, but actually it's pet dander that will inflame your eyes and make your nose run. Fortunately, the procedures for preventing or cleaning up pet hair in the home often reduce the amount of dander present as well. See Chapter 6 for more about cleaning and allergies.

VACUUM YOUR PET To people who have pets that go berserk at the merest glimpse of the vacuum cleaner, this is going to sound insane. But you really can vacuum dogs—and even cats—to prevent their hair from decorating your house. You can buy pet vacu-ums that have special grooming attachments, or use a conventional vacuum with the upholstery attachment, says Lisa Peterson, a spokesperson for the American Kennel Club. (Whatever you do, don't use the beater brush.)

Vacuuming your pet will be easiest on everybody's nerves if you start the practice while the animal is young so she grows up accustomed to the noise and the suction. Otherwise, you will need to introduce the vacuuming process very gradually. For instance, start by brushing your animal with the attachment—with no hose hooked to it and no vacuum cleaner in sight. The next time you brush your pet, have the vacuum cleaner turned on—but in another room. Keep moving the machine closer each time you brush until you can hook the hose to the attachment and apply light suction (on many vacuums, you can vent the hose to reduce the air flow). People swear that indoctrinated cats will come running, begging to be groomed, when they hear the vacuum cleaner turned on.

During shedding season, vacuum your pet daily. If the weather is nice, do the job outside so that escaped hair doesn't end up in your house. Otherwise, do the job on hard flooring, which is easier to clean up, says Peterson.

If you're afraid the vacuum cleaner will give Fido a heart attack, use one of the conventional animal brushes that are available at pet stores. When you drop that glob of fur you've collected into the trash bin, say a little prayer of thanks that this stuff isn't spread all over your furniture.

GOOD FOOD, FINE FUR Premium, nutritious pet food will give your pet the healthiest possible coat, says Rashelle Cooper, product buyer for PetSmart. A healthy coat will mean less shedding and less allergy-aggravating dander. So ask your vet what the optimum diet is for your animal.

Washing your dog frequently also will help control shedding and dander. Ask your vet what the ideal frequency is for your pet. If you do it regularly from an early age, your dog will grow up used to the process and will put up less of a fuss. Use a shampoo that's formulated for pets—not a human shampoo. For between washings, you can buy disposable wipes that promise to control shedding and dander as well.

THE SELF-CLEANING LITTER BOX

Chicago entrepreneur Alan Cook had always adroitly avoided cleaning his girlfriend's cat box. But after they were both laid up with food poisoning for a week, he could no longer ignore the stench from the neglected receptacle. He was horrified by the "absolutely disgusting" cleaning chore.

"I asked myself: We can put people on the moon—why can't we make a litter box that cleans itself?" he says.

Thus began a year's worth of research. There were some mechanized cat boxes on the market, and he began to analyze their failings. He spoke with customers in the pet aisle of the supermarket. He huddled with buddies from MIT and NASA. The result of his investigation: The ScoopFree™

self-cleaning litter box. The unit comes in two parts: the main casing, which plugs into an outlet, and a cartridge that lies under the casing and contains super-absorbent litter crystals. An infra-red sensor alerts the box when there's a cat "customer" using the litter. A timer starts, and 20 minutes later—assuming the cat doesn't return—a motorized rake drags through the litter and pulls any solids into a closed compartment, where the poop will dry out and shrink without releasing odors.

There's nothing to clean and nothing to dismantle. You just pull out the old cartridge, throw it in the trash, and replace it with a new one periodically (every 20 days to 30 days if you have one cat, and every 10 days to 15 days if you have two). An automated cat box would be particularly beneficial for elderly people or children if you have doubts about their ability to handle a conventional cat box. "It's the Swiffer principle for the litter box," Cook says.

Most cats do a good job of cleaning themselves, although there are plenty of cat shampoos and other cat-cleaning products to be found in your local pet store, too.

ERECT SOME BARRIERS Peterson uses several coverup strategies to put a barrier between her pets and her furnishings. Because her dogs like to sleep on her bed, she covers the bed with an old, tight-weave sheet to protect it from loose hair and dirt. Throw rugs and runners protect her nice carpet from hair, dirt, and doggie accidents—particularly in high-traffic areas. (She can roll the throw rugs up and stow them in a closet when guests come.) In the car, Peterson prefers leather upholstery, which pet hair will not stick to. Manufacturers offer seat covers that will protect your upholstery, too, but Peterson says it's not safe to let your pet roam freely in the car. She uses heavy plastic airline crates for her animals. You also can buy grates that will confine your pet to the cargo area of an SUV, plus protective covers for the floor of the cargo area.

TOOLS TO THE RESCUE To remove pet hair from upholstered furniture, pull on a pair of latex gloves, dampen them, and sweep your hands over the upholstery. The hair will bunch up and then is easy to remove with your fingers. Brush any excess hair off your gloves into the trash can, or rinse it off in the sink. Specialized tools are available at your pet store for the removal of pet hair, too, including squeegee-like wands and velvety mitts.

To pluck pet hair off your clothing, tear off 8 inches of packing tape, wrap it around your fingers sticky side out, and pat at the offending hair.

PUT WIPES EVERYWHERE If your dog or cat is your best friend, then disposable wipes are a close second. Station a cylinder of wipes in your bathroom, your kitchen, at each door, and in the glove box of your car. They'll be handy not only for quick hair cleanups but also to clean off paws as your pets come in the door. If you have large dogs, keep old towels near the door for wiping wet or muddy feet.

Speaking of paws, Peterson says they'll pick up less dirt in the first place if you trim the fur between and around your dog's toes with a small pair of scissors. Shorter toenails on your pet also pick up less dirt, so keep them clipped.

DOES FIDO PASS THE SNIFF TEST?

One of the great mysteries of the universe is why dogs like to roll around in certain disgusting substances they find outside. If your dog is suddenly sporting a new manure-like fragrance, a bath might be all that he needs. If the foul odor persists, however, consult a veterinarian. A number of medical maladies produce foul odors, including skin, ear, dental, and anal problems.

Inside the house, dog beds and other favorite hangouts (your nicest couch, probably) are known to develop a funky odor over time. A number of spray and powder fabric fresheners are available in pet stores and supermarkets—choose an odor-absorbing product rather than a perfumey one that will just add to the stink. Also available: sacks of odor-absorbing chemical that you can hang in pet areas to keep them smelling fresh.

Cats add their own brand of stench to a household. You might be tempted to mount a regular household air freshener near your cat's litter box, but that could have disastrous consequences. Cats are notoriously finicky about odors, and if they are driven away from the litter box, they're going to find alternative places to pee and poop—none of them fun for you. For the same reason, don't use strong-smelling cleaners on your cat box. Warm water and dishwashing liquid will clean it nicely.

To keep your cats happy and odors down, scoop the waste out of the litter box into a plastic bag every day, tie it off, and throw it into your outdoor garbage can. (The plastic has not been made that can totally contain this brand of stench, so get it out of the house.) You also have to totally replace the litter with a certain frequency. If you're using as many litter boxes as you have cats (recommended), then clay litter will need changing at least twice a week, and the modern clumping litters can stretch for 2 weeks or 3 weeks. So in the name of cheating, see if your kitty will go for the newfangled stuff.

To make the changing process simple and to keep the inside of the box clean, use a plastic litter box liner with a drawstring top. You just lift the whole mess out of the pan, throw it away, and install a new liner. (Perform this air-fouling operation outside if possible.) Before you put fresh litter into the box, pour a thin layer of baking soda into the bottom. This will help absorb odors without repelling Muffy. Or cruise the aisles of your local pet store, where you'll find any number of other nonoffensive products for absorbing cat box odors, including sprays and granules that you sprinkle over the litter.

Now you're ready. With a little training, some modest expenditures, and a few crafty measures to throw a barrier between you and the nasty stuff, you can embrace your beloved youngsters and pets without fear. Ain't love grand!

Index

A

Ackley, Shannon, 86, 92
Air, managing smells and
    pollutants in, 108–116, 214, 227–29
Air filters, 114, 206
Allergies, preventing causes of, 97,
    99–101, 111–113, 223
Aluminum foil, keeping pans clean with,
    64
Anxiety-inducing Luxuries (AILments),
    9–10
Appliances, 22, 73, 74, 76–78
Armentrout, Jennifer, 64, 70
Armoires, 38

B

Baby wipes, 17
Bacteria, disinfecting surfaces, 57–62
Barbecue grill, cleaning/care of, 188
Barco, Alexander, 155
Barry, Chris, 183
Bathrooms:
    quick cleaning routines for, 19–20,
        58, 79–81
    sanitizing strategies for, 79–82
Beckwith, Sandra, 44, 45, 46,
    48, 49, 50, 53, 55
Bedrooms, 96–102, 215–16
Beds, 7, 49, 96–97, 98, 114
Benches, storage in, 38–39
Better, Illusion, Time Saving, Economical
    (BITE), purchasing criteria of, 12
Bleach, 112–113
Blenders, 76
*Book of No, The: 250 Ways to Say It—and
    Mean It* (Newman), 46
Boorstein, Steve, clothing care strategies
    by, 123, 124, 125, 126, 127, 128, 129,
    130, 131, 136, 138, 139, 140, 144, 145
Braun, Cynthia, cleaning solutions by 14,
    73, 81, 89, 90, 91, 92, 95, 109

Brown, Pamela, 126, 134, 135
Bubble gum, removing, 177
Buckets, 16
Burling, Dorothy, 187

C

Cabinets, 22
Carpet, 96, 97, 221–23
Cars, keeping clean and tidy,
    6, 7, 191–210
Car washes, 193, 194, 195
Cats, keeping clean and odor-free with,
    221, 224, 226, 228–29
Cawley, C. Lee, organizing/cleaning
    solutions by, 27, 28, 31, 37, 82, 88,
    101, 105, 131, 132, 135, 214
CDs, organizing, 31, 33
Children:
    helping with cleaning chores, 51–55
    keeping clean and organized with,
        22, 34, 54, 211–29
    modifying cleaning routines with, 215
    storage options for, 216–18
Cleaners, types of, 17, 57, 175, 183, 184,
    185, 222–23
Cleaning:
    cheating approaches to, 6, 9
    cooking and, 67–74
    gender differences about,
        43, 44–51
    getting help with, 43–44, 51–55,
        215–18
    hiring professionals for, 50–51, 52
    real world goals for, 5–10
    technology for, 2, 11–12
Cleaning stations, 9, 13–14, 32
Cleaning tools:
    basic checklist for, 9, 13–17, 57, 58
    technological advances in, 11–12, 14
Closets, 9, 34, 101–102, 145
Clothing:
    easy-care strategies for, 6,
        53, 122–28, 141–42
    storage of, 101–102, 145,
        146, 214